## 2 Forming the tense

Put the verbs into the correct tense.

1  Lisbet's parents **weren't born** (not born) in the US.

2  Lisbet and her family _____ (go) to the beach every day.

3  In the picture, Lisbet _____ (surf) at the beach.

4  Miguel's father _____ (work) in IT.

5  'I _____ (work) for my father after the course,' says Miguel.

6  In the picture, Miguel _____ (sit) on his motorbike.

7  Fay _____ (not work) with Tom.

8  'I _____ (act) in a production of *Hamlet* next year,' says Tom.

9  In the picture, Tom and Fay _____ (walk) by the river.

## 3 Verb forms

Choose the correct form of the verb. (Circle) the correct answer.

1  She's very clever. She ___ three languages.
   a  's speaking    b  speak    (c) speaks

2  'Would you like a cigarette?' 'No, thanks. I ___.'
   a  don't smoke    b  no smoke    c  not smoking

3  I ___ to the cinema yesterday evening.
   a  go    b  gone    c  went

4  Where ___ in Argentina?
   a  you stayed    b  you stay    c  did you stay

5  My weekend was very boring. I ___ anything.
   a  didn't do    b  didn't    c  not do

6  This is a great party! Everyone ___ a good time.
   a  has    b  having    c  's having

7  'What ___ tonight?' 'I'm going out with friends.'
   a  are you doing    b  you do    c  do you do

8  I don't know this word. What ___?
   a  does it mean    b  means it    c  does mean

9  Next year I ___ study at university.
   a  'm going to    b  goes    c  go

# Questions

## 4 Auxiliaries

Put the words on the right in the correct place in the questions.

1  Where *is* Maria from?                                    **is**

2  Where you going?                                          **are**

3  What language she speaking?                               **is**

4  What you doing tonight?                                   **are**

5  Where you buy your jeans?                                 **did**

6  What you going to cook for dinner?                        **are**

7  How much money he have?                                   **does**

8  You go to work yesterday?                                 **did**

## 5 Make the question

Complete the questions.

1  'What**'s** Anna **doing**?'
   'She's reading in her bedroom.'

2  'What kind of cake _____ he _____?'
   'He's going to make a chocolate cake.'

3  'Where _____ Jane and Peter _____?'
   'They live in a flat.'

4  '_____ they _____ a car?'
   'No, they don't.'

5  'Where _____ you _____ on holiday?'
   'I'm going to Italy.'

6  'What _____ you _____ last night?'
   'I watched the football.'

7  'Where _____ your grandmother _____?'
   'She was born in London.'

8  'When _____ she _____?'
   'She got married in 1975.'

## 6 Question words

Complete the conversation with question words.

**Dad** Morning, Kate. [1] **How** are you today?

**Kate** Fine, thanks. A bit tired.

**Dad** I didn't hear you come home last night. [2] _What_ time did you get in?

**Kate** About 11.00.

**Dad** [3] _Where_ did you go?

**Kate** Just round to Beth's house.

**Dad** Oh! There's a letter for you.

**Kate** [4] _Who_'s it from?

**Dad** I don't know. Open it and see.

**Kate** Oh!

**Dad** [5] _What_'s the matter?

**Kate** Nothing … It's from Marco in Italy.

**Dad** Really? What does he say?

**Kate** He's coming to England.

**Dad** [6] _Why_?

**Kate** Because he's going to learn English.

**Dad** [7] _What_ school is he going to?

**Kate** He doesn't know yet.

**Dad** [8] _When_'s he coming?

**Kate** Next week.

**Dad** [9] _Why_ don't you invite him here for lunch on Sunday?

**Kate** OK, I will. Thanks, Dad.

## 7 Questions and answers

Match a question in **A** with an answer in **B**.

| A |
|---|
| 1 What do you do? |
| 2 Who did you go out with? |
| 3 Where do you live? |
| 4 When's your birthday? |
| 5 Why are you wearing a suit? |
| 6 How many students are there? |
| 7 How much did you pay for it? |
| 8 How are you? |
| 9 Which search engine do you use? |
| 10 Whose is this money? |

| B | | |
|---|---|---|
| a | 7 | £45. |
| b | 6 | 16. |
| c | | Fine, thanks. And you? |
| d | 2 | My friend Paul. |
| e | 1 | I'm a teacher. |
| f | 9 | Google. |
| g | 4 | April 22nd. |
| h | 10 | It's mine. Thanks. |
| i | 3 | In a flat in town. |
| j | 5 | I'm going to a wedding. |

## 8 *who's* or *whose*?

Complete the sentences with *who's* or *whose*.

1 '_Who's_ going to the cinema on Saturday?'
'Everyone except Tom.'

2 '_Whose_ is that beautiful coat?'
'It's Olivia's. It cost £200!'

3 '_Whose_ bag is this?'
'It's mine.'

4 '_Who's_ that knocking at the door?'
'No idea. I'll go and see.'

5 '_Who's_ that beautiful girl with Pete?'
'It's Jane. She's his younger sister.'

6 'Do you know _whose_ house that is?'
'Yes, Mr Richards lives there.'

Fourth edition

# New Headway

**Pre-Intermediate** Workbook with key

John and Liz Soars

with **iChecker** CD-ROM

Assess › Progress

OXFORD

UNIVERSITY PRESS

# Contents

See **iChecker** CD-ROM for **AUDIO BANK**, **UNIT TESTS**, and **LINKS**

# 1

Tense revision • Questions • Right word, wrong word
• Pronunciation – vowel sounds

**Getting to know you**

## Tense revision

**1 Present, past, and future**

Complete the texts with the verb forms in the box.

**1**

| |
|---|
| ~~live~~ |
| ~~didn't like~~ |
| ~~were~~ born |
| ~~love~~ |
| ~~moved~~ |
| 'm going to study |
| ~~go~~ |
| ~~'m taking~~ |

### Lisbet, from the US

'Hi! My name's Lisbet, and I'm from Santa Barbara, California. I [1] **live** with my parents and my sisters in a house near the sea. We [2] _go_ to the beach every day. We all [3] _love_ surfing!

I'm American, but my parents [4] _were born_ in Norway. They [5] _moved_ to the US 20 years ago. They [6] _didn't like_ the cold winters in Norway!

I'm in my final year at school. I [7] _'m taking_ exams at the moment. Next year I [8] _'m going to study_ Marine Biology at university.'

**2**

| |
|---|
| 's going to work |
| ~~comes~~ |
| didn't start |
| likes |
| 's studying |
| ~~has~~ |
| gave |
| 'm enjoying |

### Miguel, from Spain

This is Miguel. He [1] _comes_ from Spain. He's a student at the EAE Business School in Madrid, where he [2] _has_ International Law. 'I [3] _____ the course a lot,' he says. 'It's really interesting.' After the course he [4] _____ for his father's IT company.

He [5] _____ a motorbike, and he [6] _____ racing it at the weekend. He [7] _____ riding until he was 16. His father [8] _____ him a bike for his birthday. 'Going fast is my passion!' he says.

**3**

| |
|---|
| acts |
| live |
| don't work |
| went |
| made |
| 's doing |
| didn't win |
| prefer |

### Tom and Fay, from England

Tom and Fay Dickens [1] _____ in Bristol with their two children. They're both actors, but they [2] _____ together. Fay [3] _____ in films, and Tom works in the theatre. 'I [4] _____ the excitement of the theatre,' says Tom.

Last year Fay [5] _____ to Hollywood. 'I [6] _____ a film with Steven Spielberg,' she says. 'It was good, but it [7] _____ any awards!'

Next year Tom [8] _____ a tour of Britain in a production of *Hamlet*. Tom is playing the title role. 'I'm very excited about it,' he says.

# Vocabulary

## 9 Right word, wrong word

**1** Choose the correct verb for each line.

**play   go**

1 Do you want to **play** a game?

I try to **go** swimming at least once a week.

**do   make**

2 Good luck in the exam! _do_ your best!

I _make_ my own bread every morning.

**say   tell**

3 You must always _tell_ the truth.

I always _say_ 'hello' when I see her.

**watch   look**

4 Can I have a _look_ at the photos of your wedding?

Did you _watch_ the match last night?

**lend   borrow**

5 Can I _borrow_ some money? I'll give it back to you tomorrow.

Jack is going to _lend_ us his car for the weekend.

**2** Underline two nouns that go with the adjective.

1 beautiful          <u>woman</u> / meal / <u>picture</u>

2 interesting        phone / <u>book</u> / <u>film</u>

3 exciting           teacher / <u>story</u> / <u>film</u>

4 strong             <u>man</u> / <u>coffee</u> / exam

5 handsome           <u>man</u> / <u>boy</u> / view

**3** Complete the sentences with the correct preposition.

in   for (x3)   at (x2)   to   with   of (x2)

1 I'm waiting **for** the postman to arrive.

2 Look _at_ that picture! Isn't it beautiful!

3 I'm looking _for_ Mary. Is she here?

4 Are you good _at_ maths?

5 This book is full _of_ useful information.

6 Are you interested _in_ history?

7 You're so right. I agree _with_ you.

8 My brother works _for_ Barclays Bank.

9 Can I speak _to_ you for a minute?

10 I'm afraid _of_ dogs.

**4** Complete each pair of sentences with the correct word.

kind   ~~train~~   left   rest   flat

1 When's the next **train** to London?

Athletes **train** every day to keep fit.

2 You look tired. You need to _rest_ more.

We had lunch and spent the _rest_ of the day on the beach.

3 Holland is a very _flat_ country. There are no mountains.

I live in a _flat_ in the centre of town.

4 A present? For me? How _kind_ of you!

What _kind_ of music do you like?

5 Turn _left_ at the end of the street.

We _left_ for the airport at 6.30.

## Reading

### 10 Janice and Andy

1 🎧 Read the interview with Janice. Write the questions in the correct place in the text.

> How many children do you have?
> ~~Where did you meet?~~
> What does Andy do?
> Where did you go on your first date?
> What do you like doing together?
> When and where did you get married?
> ~~Was it love at first sight?~~
> Where are you going on your next holiday?

2 Answer the questions.

1 Did Janice like the boy she was at the party with?

_Where did you meet_

2 How did she feel when she saw Andy for the first time?

_attracted_

3 Where did they go on their first date?

_____

4 Why did she like their wedding?

_____

5 How did the arrival of the twins change their relationship?

_____

6 Why does Andy travel in his job?

_____

7 What do they like doing together?

_____

8 Where are they going on holiday?

_____

8   Unit 1 • Getting to know you

# Let's stick together

**Janice and Andy have been together for 15 years. They live in a cottage near the sea in Wales. Janice describes their relationship.**

**1   Where did you meet?**

At a party. I was 18, and it was my best friend's birthday party. There were about 50 of us in a club. I wasn't having a very good time. I was with another boy, and he was so annoying – I didn't really want to be with him.

**2   _Was it love at first sight_ ?**

I saw Andy across the room, and I was immediately attracted to him. When our eyes met, it was like a light going on between us. I knew straightaway that he was the one for me, and luckily he felt the same way.

**3   _Where did you go on your first date_ ?**

We went to a gig. His friend was in a band, and we went to see them. They played till midnight, and we danced and danced. Andy was a terrible dancer, but it didn't put me off him.

**4   _When and where did you get married_ ?**

We got married three years later in a small church near my parents' house. We didn't have much money at the time, so it was a very small wedding. We just invited a few close friends and relatives, but it was very romantic.

# Listening

## 11 Andy and Ed

1 🎧 Listen to Andy talking to his colleague, Ed. Answer the questions.

1 Why is Ed a bit nervous?

_____

2 What's Andy's secret for a happy marriage?

_____

3 How old was Andy when he met Janice?

_____

4 Who was bored? Who was boring?

_____

5 When did Janice and Andy leave the party?

_____

6 What do Andy and Janice have in common?

_____

7 What couldn't Janice do after the twins were born?

_____

8 How many guests are going to Ed's wedding?

_____

5 _____ ?

Two – Tamzin and Jessica. They're twins, and they're eight years old. When they were born it changed the whole relationship. Until they arrived, we were kids. After they arrived, we were proper grown-ups.

6 _____ ?

He's a music producer. He works in a recording studio. He helps bands produce the sound they're looking for. He travels abroad a lot. Bands like recording in sunny places like Jamaica!

7 _____ ?

Making music. He plays the guitar, and I sing. We sometimes do little gigs together at weddings or pubs, just for friends. Other than that, it's ordinary things like playing with the kids or going to the cinema – if we can get a babysitter!

8 _____ ?

We're going to see friends in Cornwall, in the south-west of England. They live on a farm, and we're going to stay in a tent in a field on their land. We're all taking our wellies – we stayed there last year and it rained every day!

2 🎧 Listen again. Complete the sentences from Andy and Ed's conversation.

1 '… aren't you _____ married soon?'

2 'We just _____ in love.'

3 'He was a friend but not a boyfriend, if you _____ what I _____.'

4 '… we discovered that we _____, and still _____, so many things in common.'

5 '… we _____ as many gigs as before.'

6 'Janice _____ abroad with me on work trips any more.'

7 'Are you _____ a big wedding?'

8 'I _____ my wedding a lot.'

# Pronunciation

## 12 Vowel sounds

> Most phonetic symbols for vowels are easy to understand.
>
> /ɪ/ bit    /iː/ see    /e/ bed
>
> Some are a little more difficult.
>
> /æ/ hat    /ʌ/ sun    /ɑː/ father    /ɒ/ hot
>
> /ʊ/ put    /ɔː/ sort    /ɜː/ learn
>
> ▶▶ **Phonetic symbols p102**

**1** Write a word in **B** next to the phonetic symbols in **A**.

| A | | B |
|---|---|---|
| 1 /kɑː(r)/ __car__ | | ~~foot~~ |
| 2 /fʊt/ _Foot_ | | mean |
| 3 /fʌn/ _fun_ | | ~~ear~~ |
| 4 /kæt/ _cat_ | | win |
| 5 /miːn _mean_ | | work |
| 6 /wɜːk/ _walk_ | | ~~fun~~ |
| 7 /wɪn/ _win_ | | ~~cat~~ |
| 8 /wɔːk/ _work_ | | walk |

🎧 Listen and check.

> Some words have the same pronunciation but a different spelling and a different meaning.
>
> /siː/ sea and see    /njuː/ new and knew

**2** 🎧 Write the other word that has the same phonetic symbols.

1 /tuː/     two and __too__

2 /miːt/     meet and _meat_

3 /fɔː(r)/     for and _four_

4 /sʌn/     sun and _son_

5 /bɔːd/     bored and _board_

6 /piːs/     piece and _pics_

**3** 🎧 Write the correct spelling.

1 I have /tuː/ __two__ /sʌnz/ __sons__ .

2 I like your /njuː/ _new_ shoes.

3 Would you like a /piːs/ _pics_ of cake with your coffee?

4 I'm /bɔːd/ _bored_ . I want to go home.

5 I don't eat /miːt/ _meat_!

## *Just for fun!*

## 13 Words that rhyme

Find the pairs of words that rhyme.

good ~~learn~~ meal   food   ~~caught~~ steak   saw ~~busy~~

make ~~rude~~   turn fizzy ~~sort~~   feel ~~could~~ more

| learn | turn |
|---|---|
| caught | could |
| busy | rude |
| learn | sort |

## 14 Crossword – opposite adjectives

Complete the crossword with the opposite of the adjectives in the clues.

**Across**

3 same (9)
5 full (5)
6 first (4)
10 correct (5)
11 interesting (6)
12 cheap (9)

**Down**

1 noisy (5)
2 early (4)
4 lovely (8)
7 married (6)
8 clever (6)
9 best (5)

## 2

Present tenses • Spelling • Gerunds and -ing forms
• have/have got • Pronunciation – 's at the end of a word

**Whatever makes you happy**

# Present Simple

## 1 Positive, negative, question

**1** Complete the text with the verb forms in the box.

| works | don't feel | ~~live~~ | has | doesn't earn | prefer |
|-------|------------|----------|-----|--------------|--------|
| don't have | need | work | have | doesn't matter | goes |

### Living in the country

Dave Clarke is a sheep farmer in New Zealand. He and his wife [1] **live** in a farmhouse in the hills with their two children. Dave [2] _has_ 600 sheep. He [3] _work_ seven days a week and at least ten hours a day.

'We [4] _don't have_ any days off,' says Dave. 'The animals [5] _need_ feeding every day. In lambing season we [6] _work_ all night, too!'

Once a month he [7] _____ to the market in the nearby town to buy or sell sheep. 'I [8] _don't feel_ comfortable in towns. I [9] _prefer_ being in the countryside. I feel free here.'

Dave [10] _____ a lot – about $40,000 a year, but, as he says, 'Money is important, but it [11] _doesn't matter_ that much to me. I'm very lucky. I [12] _have_ the best job in the world!'

**2** Complete the questions about Dave.

1 'What **does** Dave **do** ?'
  'He's a sheep farmer.'

2 'Where _____ Dave and his wife _____?'
  'In a farmhouse in the hills.'

3 'How many sheep _____ he _____?'
  '600.'

4 'How many hours a week _____ he _____?'
  'At least 70.'

5 'Why _____ he _____ to the market?'
  'To buy or sell sheep.'

6 'How much _____ he _____?'
  'About $40,000 a year.'

**3** Complete the negative sentences.

1 Dave **doesn't have** (not have) any days off.

2 They _____ (not go) to bed in lambing season.

3 He _____ (not like) being in towns.

4 'I _____ (not earn) a lot, but it _____ (not matter).'

**4** Write the short answers.

1 'Do Dave and his wife have any children?' '**Yes, they do** .'

2 'Does he have any days off?' '_____.'

3 'Does he like being in the countryside?' '_____?'

4 'Do you earn a lot, Dave?' '_____.'

5 'Do you like your job, Dave?' '_____.'

## 2 State verbs

Complete the sentences with the verbs in the box in the correct form.

| need | belong | cost | not understand | have | ~~not know~~ |
|------|--------|------|----------------|------|----------|
| think | like | agree | not matter | mean | prefer |

1 I __don't know__ the answer to this question. Can you help me?

2 What _____ you _____ of my new car? Do you like it?

3 He has a very strong accent. I _____ him.

4 I'm going to the shops. ____ you _____ anything?

5 Who does this coat _____ to? Is it yours?

6 This café is very expensive! A sandwich _____ £5!

7 'I'm sorry I'm late.' 'It _____. Don't worry.'

8 I don't know this word. Can you tell me what it _____?

9 England _____ a population of over 50 million people.

10 'This government is rubbish!' 'I _____. They're terrible.'

11 '____ you _____ ice cream?' 'I love it.'

12 Which do you _____ – the red or the blue shirt?

## 3 Adverbs of frequency

Put the words in the correct order.

1 cinema/I/to/often/go/friends/my/with/the

__I often go to the cinema with my friends.__

2 have/toast/usually/I/breakfast/for

_____

3 always/TV/morning/watch/I/the/in

_____

4 holiday/often/how/do/have/you/a?

_____

5 sometimes/we/Japanese/go/a/restaurant/to

_____

6 school/I/late/never/for/am

_____

# Spelling

## 4 Third person -s

Write the third person singular of these verbs.

1 live      __lives__

2 work      _____

3 enjoy     _____

4 play      _____

5 go        _____

6 do        _____

7 have      _____

8 watch     _____

9 finish    _____

10 relax    _____

11 study    _____

12 try      _____

## 5 -ing

Write the -ing form of these verbs.

1 rain      __raining__

2 go        _____

3 come      _____

4 have      _____

5 take      _____

6 leave     _____

7 swim      _____

8 run       _____

9 stop      _____

10 begin    _____

11 travel   _____

12 hit      _____

rain

raining

# Present Simple and Continuous

## 6 *What does he do?/What's he doing?*

Look at the pictures and answer the questions.

I'm Tom. I'm a teacher.

1 What does Tom do?

He's a teacher.

2 Where does he work?

he works in a school.

3 Is he teaching now?

Yes he is

I'm Laura. I'm an actress.

4 What does Laura do?

She is an actress

5 Where does she work?

She work in a theatre.

6 Is she acting now?

Yes she is

7 What's she doing?

She is playing

## 7 Choosing the correct form

Choose the correct form of the verb. (Circle) the correct answer.

1 I ___ to work now. See you later.

   (**a** 'm going)   **b** go

2 We ___ the news on TV every evening.

   **a** 're watching   (**b** watch)

3 Don't turn the TV off! I ___ it!

   **a** watch   (**b** 'm watching)

4 Maria's Italian. She ___ from Milan.

   **a** 's coming   (**b** comes)

5 ___ Spanish food? I love tapas.

   **a** Do you like   **b** Are you liking

6 I ___ any pets.

   **a** 'm not having   **b** don't have

7 Don't wait for Peter. He ___ .

   **a** doesn't come   **b** isn't coming

8 What's the matter? Why ___ crying?

   **a** are you   **b** do you

## 8 Correct the mistakes

Correct the mistakes in these sentences.

1 I'm ~~liking~~ black coffee.   *I like*

2 The sun is rising in the east.

3 I look for a white shirt in medium. Have you got any?

4 'Where's Paul?' 'He's over there. He talks to Angela.'

5 She's 21 years old! I'm not believing her!

6 I'm learn English for my job.

7 Why you going out without a coat? It's freezing!

8 My father work in a bank.

## Reading

### 9 All you need is love

**1** 🎧 Read the article. Complete the sentences with a word from the text.

1 Money doesn't buy _____ .

2 Lottery winners were often happier _____ they won.

3 Ordinary people don't have as many _____ as rich people.

4 $45,000 a year is _____ to buy the important things in life.

5 People who earn more than $45,000 a year _____ always happier than people who earn less.

**2** Answer the questions.

1 According to James Montier, what is the secret to personal happiness?

_____

2 Why is exercise important?

_____

3 What sort of job is best?

_____

4 What are the best things to do if you can afford it?

_____

5 Why are experiences better than buying something?

_____

6 Why is it silly for the wife of a millionaire to buy her husband another car?

_____

7 What are the two things that really make us happy?

_____

# All you need is love

**'Earning more than $45,000 a year doesn't make you any happier.' Who says this? An investment banker!**

Most of us think that rich people are happy people, but research shows that money doesn't buy you happiness. Most lottery winners don't enjoy their win after the first moment of excitement. In fact, they often say they were happier before they won. When you see a photograph of a millionaire, how often are they smiling? Billionaires with ten houses and three yachts have more worries than ordinary people, and bigger bills.

A report by James Montier, who works for an investment bank, says that all you need is a salary of $45,000 a year. This is enough money to buy food, a home, clothes, and healthcare. People who earn more than this aren't necessarily any happier.

**The report also says:**

♥ Give time and energy to close relationships. This, more than anything else, is the secret to personal happiness.

♥ Look at the world around you and see what is good about it. Smell the roses. Listen to the birds.

♥ Exercise regularly. A healthy body means a healthy mind.

♥ Try to do a job you enjoy. We spend a third of our lives working.

♥ Live in the moment. Enjoy what you're doing. Don't live in the past or the future.

### The best thing to do with money

If you are lucky enough to have money, says the report, the best thing to do with it is to go on holiday with people you love or have life-changing experiences, such as walking the Himalayas or diving in the Red Sea. The memory of these experiences stays with you forever.

If you buy a new car or a designer handbag, you are excited for a very short time, and then it is no longer exciting. Think of the millionaire wife who buys her husband a new £250,000 Rolls-Royce Phantom for his birthday. He already has 15 cars. What is he going to do with the sixteenth? How many cars can he drive at the same time?

The problem is that we think that money brings happiness. But we need to remember that what makes us really happy is friends and family. As John Lennon said, '*All you need is love.*'

# Listening

## 10 The best things in life are free

**1** 🎧 Listen to the interview with the Smith family. Complete the chart with the things they like and why they like them.

| | **What?** | **Why?** |
|---|---|---|
| Ben, 8 | | |
| Kirstie, 10 | | |
| Nigel, 41 | | |
| Fiona, 38 | | |

**2** 🎧 Listen again. Complete the lines from the conversation. Who says them?

1  '… you can't have **everything** you want **when** you want it.'   **Nigel**

2  'He cost _____ because he came from the _____ home.'

3  '… she always _____ when she sees me, and she _____ out her hands for me to _____ her up.'

4  'All day long I work in the _____, _____ city, among _____ of people.'

5  '… there are _____ of things I like that _____ anything.'

6  'I find it _____ every year.'

7  'There's nothing _____ beautiful than a glorious red _____ at the end of the day.'

8  'Don't be _____ Kirstie!'

# Vocabulary

## 11 Gerunds and -ing forms

**1** Complete the sentences with the –ing form of a verb in the box.

| cook | shop | ~~have~~ | go |
|---|---|---|---|

1  **Having** a lot of money doesn't make you happy.

2  I like _____ out with my friends at the weekend.

3  _____ online is easier than driving to the supermarket.

4  I do the _____ in our family – even bread and cakes.

| download | send | make | get |
|---|---|---|---|

5  My favourite thing on Friday evening is _____ a take-away pizza.

6  _____ music from the Internet is sometimes illegal.

7  _____ new friends isn't always easy.

8  _____ emails is easier than writing a letter.

| go | mend | chat | do |
|---|---|---|---|

9  The best thing about the Internet is _____ to friends on Facebook.

10  I hate _____ nothing. I like to be busy all the time.

11  I love _____ shopping, especially for clothes.

12  Tom's good at _____ computers. He can fix almost any problem.

**2** Make a compound noun with an –ing form in **A** and a noun in **B**.

| A | | B | |
|---|---|---|---|
| swimming | ~~parking~~ | bag | list |
| sleeping | driving | machine | licence |
| shopping | washing | costume | ~~ticket~~ |

1  I parked on a double yellow line and got a £40 **parking ticket** .

2  I don't have a car because I haven't got a _____ .

3  Put all your dirty clothes in the _____ .

4  I always write a _____ before I go to the supermarket.

5  Don't forget to bring a _____ when we go camping next weekend.

6  Let's go for a swim. Have you got your _____ ?

# have/have got

## 12 Two forms

**1**  Look at the picture of the White's house. Complete the lines in two ways, once with a form of *have* and once with a form of *have got*.

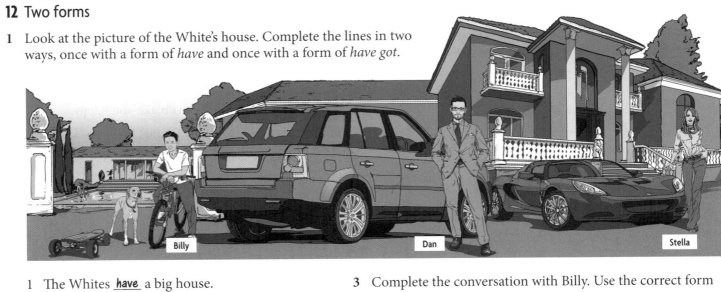

Billy    Dan    Stella

1  The Whites **have** a big house.

   The Whites **have got** a big house.

2  Dan _____ a 4x4.

   Dan _____ a 4x4.

3  Stella _____ a sportscar.

   Stella _____ a sportscar.

4  They _____ a son called Billy.

   They _____ a son called Billy.

5  'We _____ a dog called Molly.'

   'We _____ a dog called Molly.'

6  Billy _____ a mountain bike.

   Billy _____ a mountain bike.

**2**  Complete the questions and short answers.

1  '_____ Billy have a skateboard?'

   'Yes, _____.'

2  '_____ he got a mountain bike?'

   'Yes, _____.'

3  '_____ they have a cat?'

   'No, _____.'

4  '_____ Dan and Stella have their own cars?'

   'Yes, _____.'

5  '_____ they got a swimming pool?'

   'Yes, _____.'

6  '_____ you got a 4x4, Stella?'

   'No, _____. I've got a sportscar.'

**3**  Complete the conversation with Billy. Use the correct form of *have got*.

**A**  Hi, Billy. Tell me about your bedroom. [1] _____ you _____ a lot of things in your room?

**B**  I guess so. I [2] _____ a big TV and a computer.

**A**  What sort of computer [3] _____ you _____?

**B**  It's a Sony.

**A**  And I suppose you [4] _____ a PlayStation!

**B**  No, I [5] _____. I did have one, but it broke! I prefer to play real games. I love golf.

**A**  [6] _____ you _____ your own golf clubs?

**B**  No, I use dad's. He [7] _____ some really nice ones.

**4**  Rewrite the sentences using the other form of *have/have got*.

1  Do you have the time, please?

   **Have you got the time, please?**

2  I've got a terrible headache!

   _____

3  Have you got any aspirin?

   _____

4  You have a beautiful flat!

   _____

5  Sally's got a really good job.

   _____

6  I haven't got any money.

   _____

# Pronunciation

## 13  -s at the end of a word

-s appears at the end of a word in:

- **plural nouns**
  *books    trains    houses*
- ***he/she/it** + **Present Simple***
  *gets    lives    washes*
- **possessive *'s***
  *Pat's car    John's car    Liz's car*

**1** 🎧 Listen to the three different pronunciations of *-s* at the end of a word.

| /s/ | books | gets | Pat's |
|-----|-------|------|-------|
| /z/ | trains | lives | John's |
| /ɪz/ | houses | washes | Liz's |

**2** 🎧 Listen. Write the words in the correct column.

| ~~works~~ | ~~plays~~ | ~~buses~~ | Pete's | Peter's |
|-----------|-----------|-----------|--------|---------|
| loves | watches | wants | runs | languages |
| relaxes | hates | Anna's | Rick's | George's |
| tickets | starts | teachers | flats | clothes |
| pieces | rains | Henry's | goes | finishes |

| /s/ | /z/ | /ɪz/ |
|-----|-----|------|
| works | plays | buses |
|  |  |  |
|  |  |  |
|  |  |  |

**3** 🎧 Listen then practise saying the sentences.

1  Ann's sister finishes work at 3.00 on Monday afternoons.

2  It always rains on Sundays.

3  Rick's mother speaks six languages.

4  George's daughter loves clothes and horses.

5  Mary's boyfriend runs twenty miles over hills and fields.

## Just for fun!

## 14  Word wheel

Use the letters in the wheel to make nine free time activities. They all end in *–ing*. You can use the same letter twice.

dancing

singing

## 15  Crossword – plural nouns

Complete the crossword with the plural of the nouns in the clues.

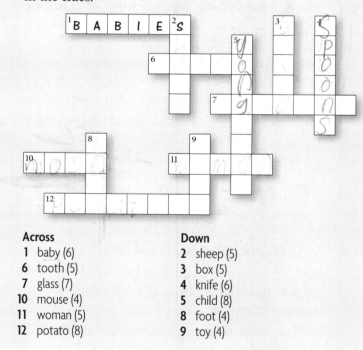

| **Across** | **Down** |
|------------|----------|
| **1** baby (6) | **2** sheep (5) |
| **6** tooth (5) | **3** box (5) |
| **7** glass (7) | **4** knife (6) |
| **10** mouse (4) | **5** child (8) |
| **11** woman (5) | **8** foot (4) |
| **12** potato (8) | **9** toy (4) |

## 3

Past Simple – regular and irregular past • Time expressions
• Past Continuous • Pronunciation – consonants
• *have* + noun = activity

**What's in the news?**

## Past Simple

**1 Positive**

Complete the text with the Past Simple form of the verbs in the boxes.

# Across the Channel in a chair

There are many ways to cross from England to France – by boat, plane or Eurostar, for example. But one man chose another form of transport.

| travel | set off | become | ~~tie~~ | reach |

**Jonathan Trappe** [1] _tied_ 54 balloons to a chair and floated across the Channel. He [2] _____ the first person to cross the Channel with balloons filled with helium.

Mr Trappe [3] _____ from an airfield near Ashford at 5 a.m. He [4] _____ a height of 1,200 metres and [5] _____ at a top speed of 40 km/h.

| plan | land | control | take | have | fly |

The journey was 22 miles, and it [6] _____ over four hours. He [7] _____ in a field in northern France. He [8] _____ his landing by cutting away some of the balloons.

He [9] _____ the trip carefully. He needed permission from aviation authorities, and he was equipped with sat-nav, a radio, and oxygen.

Mr Trappe, 36, thinks it's a wonderful way to fly. 'A gas balloon flies in complete silence,' he says. 'I could hear the waves from a height of 300 metres.'

'As a child, I always [10] _____ a dream of holding a bunch of balloons and floating away into space. Didn't everybody?'

The first balloon crossing of the Channel was in 1785. A Frenchman, Jean-Pierre Blanchard, and an American doctor, John Jefferies, [11] _____ from Dover to Calais. It took two and a half hours.

**Jonathan Trappe floats across the Channel**

## 2 Questions and negatives

**1** Write the questions about Jonathan Trappe.

1 'How _did he cross the channel?_ '

'He crossed the Channel in a chair tied to balloons.'

2 'How many balloons _____?'

'He had 54 balloons.'

3 'What time _____?'

'He set off at 5 a.m.'

4 'How fast _____?'

'He travelled at a top speed of 40 km/h.'

5 'How long _____?'

'The journey took over four hours.'

6 'Where _____?'

'He landed in a field in northern France.'

7 'What equipment _____?'

'He had sat-nav, a radio, and oxygen.'

8 'When _____?'

'The first balloon crossing was in 1785.'

**2** Correct the information in these sentences.

1 Jonathan sat in a basket.

_He didn't sit in a basket. He sat in a chair._

2 He set off from his garden.

_____

3 He started his journey at 5.00 in the afternoon.

_____

4 He flew at 500 metres.

_____

5 The journey was 50 miles.

_____

**3** Answer the questions with short answers.

1 'Did he cross the Channel by boat?' _'No, he didn't.'_

2 'Did he sit in a chair?' '_____'

3 'Did he land in the sea?' '_____'

4 'Did he need permission to make the trip?' '_____'

5 'Did John Jefferies cross the Channel in 1785?' '_____'

## 3 Regular and irregular verbs

**1** Write the Past Simple of these verbs.

1 study _studied_
  try _____
  hurry _____

2 die _____
  live _____
  arrive _____

3 plan _____
  stop _____
  travel _____

4 make _____
  feel _____
  send _____
  know _____

**2** Which of these past tense verbs rhyme? Tick (✓) the pairs that rhyme. Cross (✗) the pairs that don't.

1 paid said ✗
2 saw wore ✓
3 cut put ☐
4 read said ☐
5 heard made ☐
6 could stood ☐
7 broke took ☐
8 ate met ☐
9 won ran ☐
10 bought caught ☐

🎧 Listen and check.

# Time expressions

## 4 Saying when

**1** Complete the time expressions with *in*, *at*, or *on*.

| | | | |
|---|---|---|---|
| 1 | **on** Sunday | 7 | ____ Christmas |
| 2 | ____ 2010 | 8 | ____ April |
| 3 | ____ 8.00 | 9 | ____ the morning |
| 4 | ____ winter | 10 | ____ night |
| 5 | ____ Monday morning | 11 | ____ the 1990s |
| 6 | ____ the weekend | 12 | ____ midnight |

**2** Write *last* before the noun or *ago* after the noun.

| | | | |
|---|---|---|---|
| 1 | **last** week | — |
| 2 | _____ night | _____ |
| 3 | _____ a week | _____ |
| 4 | _____ ten years | _____ |
| 5 | _____ year | _____ |
| 6 | _____ two months | _____ |

**3** Complete the conversation with words from the box.

| in (x2) | at (x2) | on (x3) | last | ago | when |
|---|---|---|---|---|---|

**A** When's your birthday?

**B** ¹ **In** September.

**A** What day?

**B** It's ² ____ the 13th.

**A** What year were you born?

**B** I was born ³ ____ 1991. When's your birthday?

**A** It was a couple of weeks ⁴ ____, actually. It was my birthday ⁵ ____ the 7th.

**B** Really? What did you do ⁶ ____ your birthday?

**A** Not much. ⁷ ____ I was 21, I had a huge party with fireworks ⁸ ____ midnight, and ⁹ ____ year we went to a club, but this year was very quiet.

**B** Well, we're having a party for Sally's birthday. It's next Saturday ¹⁰ ____ 8.00. Do you want to come?

**A** Great! I'd love to!

# Past Continuous

## 5 Making the Past Continuous

**1** This is what you saw when you arrived at work yesterday. Write sentences in the Past Continuous.

*When I arrived at work …*

1 Dave and Ellie/chat/next to photocopier

   **Dave and Ellie were chatting next to the photocopier.**

2 Penny/eat/a cake

   _____

3 Martin/drink/coffee

   _____

4 Sally/shop/online

   _____

5 Rob and Matt/talk/about last night's match

   _____

**2** Complete the questions.

1 'Who _____ Dave _____ to?' 'Ellie.'

2 'What _____ Penny _____?' 'A cake.'

3 'What _____ you _____, Sally?' 'A new dress.'

4 'What _____ you _____ to Matt about, Rob?' 'The match.'

**3** Complete the negative sentences.

1 Martin **wasn't drinking** (not drink) tea.

2 Dave and Ellie _____ (not use) the photocopier.

3 Sally _____ (not do) any work.

4 Rob and Matt _____ (not talk) about work.

## 6 News stories

Read the three news stories. Put the phrases in the box in the correct place in the stories.

1  ... while he was swimming ...
2  ... , who was digging in his garden, ...
3  ... who was driving dangerously, ...
4  ... as I was planting potatoes
5  ... , where his parents were waiting for him
6  ... because he was going to visit his mother

### a Channel Champion

Twelve-year-old James White became one of the youngest people to swim the English Channel when he completed the 21-mile crossing yesterday. The journey took him just under 12 hours to complete. He drank hot soup _1_ because he felt so cold in the water. 'The most difficult part was avoiding all the boats,' said James. He was exhausted but proud when he finally reached the coast of France __ .

James White, 12

### b Blind driver arrested

Police in Kentucky stopped a 31-year-old man, Daniel McCarthy, __ and then discovered that he was blind. 'He had his dog with him,' said police spokesman Melvyn Kittburg. McCarthy said he only recently lost his sight.

He knew the road very well __ . His dog was trained to bark once at a red light and twice at a green light. McCarthy lost his driving licence.

### c MAN FINDS ROMAN COINS

A pensioner __ found a pot that contained over a thousand silver coins. Experts said that the coins dated from the third century AD, when the Emperor Carausius ruled ancient Britain. The pensioner, Mr Alfred Perkins, explained 'My spade hit something hard __ . It's so exciting to hold a coin in your hand that someone used to buy bread nearly 2,000 years ago.'

## 7 Past Simple or Continuous?

Write the verb once in the Past Simple and once in the Past Continuous.

**have**

1  'I went to Harry's party last night.'
   ' _Did_ you _have_ a good time?'

2  They _were having_ dinner when the phone rang.

**rain**

3  When I left the house, it _____ , so I took my umbrella.

4  'Did you have good weather for your wedding?'
   'No, it _____ all day, but it didn't matter.'

**talk**

5  You were on the phone for ages!
   Who _____ you _____ to?

6  I had a problem with my neighbour, but I _____ to him, and it's OK now.

**wear**

7  When I saw Bella, she _____ a beautiful red dress – she looked stunning.

8  'What _____ you _____ for your interview yesterday?'
   'A suit and tie.'

**live**

9  I _____ in Rome when I was a child.

10  I _____ in Rome when I met my first wife.

## Reading

### 8 Caught in the act

**1** 🎧 Read the newspaper article. (Circle) the correct answer.

1 John Pearce is …
   a the owner.    b the burglar.    c a neighbour.

2 Paul Ives is …
   a the owner.    b the burglar.    c a neighbour.

3 Nicola Daniels is …
   a the owner.    b the burglar.    c a neighbour.

4 The burglar thought it was an easy job because …
   a the window was open.
   b there was no one at home.

5 He got stuck …
   a while he was leaving the house.
   b while he was entering the house.

**2** Answer the questions.

1 What did the neighbours do when they saw the burglar?

_____

2 How did the burglar try to explain the situation?

_____

3 Who got John Pearce down from the window?

_____

4 What did Nicola Daniels think the noise was at first?

_____

5 Why didn't anyone want to help the burglar?

_____

**3** Find a word or words in the article that mean …

1 rude or unkind words          _abuse_
2 with the top part at the bottom  _____
3 broken into many pieces       _____
4 not able to move              _____
5 unable to escape             _____
6 shouting very loudly          _____
7 loud knocking                _____

# Caught in the act

**Crowd shouts abuse as burglar is stuck hanging upside down**

**John Pearce**, a 32-year-old burglar, thought he had another easy job as he was breaking into an empty house.

He smashed the window of the house in Dartford, Kent, with a hammer. But while he was climbing in through the smashed window, his foot got stuck, and he couldn't free himself.

He was hanging upside down in the window for more than three hours while neighbours laughed and shouted at him.

When the owner of the house, **Paul Ives**, arrived home from work, he didn't understand why people were standing outside his house. Then he saw the burglar trapped in his own window. Paul said, 'He kept saying, "I haven't done anything. I was stopping the burglars".'

Unsurprisingly, Mr Ives didn't believe him. Police arrived at the scene and got him down. He was arrested and taken to the police station.

Mr Ives, 44, an engineer, said, 'He must be the world's worst burglar. He was screaming at everyone to get him down, and we were all saying "I don't think so".'

Next-door neighbour, **Nicola Daniels**, 34, said, 'I heard banging and thought Paul and his girlfriend were moving furniture. When the banging continued, I looked out of the window and saw this man hanging upside down. He was swearing and shouting "I'm not the burglar!".'

'Another neighbour called the police, and there was quite a crowd standing and laughing at him. It was his own fault. He deserved it all.'

## Listening

**9 Someone stole my bag!**

🎧 Listen to the conversation. Someone has stolen Mrs Clements' bag, and she is at the police station. (Circle) the correct answers.

1 Margot Clements was walking in *the town / a park*.

2 She was carrying her jacket in her *left / right* hand.

3 She couldn't find her *bag / mobile phone*.

4 She lives at *13 / 30* Marlins *Close / Road*.

5 The thief had long *blonde / brown* hair and blue *eyes / jeans*.

6 The theft happened at *one o'clock / twenty past one*.

7 Her bag was *quite / very* big and *green / grey* and black.

8 Her purse had *£15 / £50* and her *car / house* keys in it.

9 The police *caught / didn't catch* the thief.

## Pronunciation

**10 Consonants**

Most phonetic symbols for consonants are easy to understand.

| /g/ *get* | /h/ *hot* | /m/ *my* |
|---|---|---|

Some are more difficult.

| /θ/ thief | /ð/ there | /ʃ/ shirt |
|---|---|---|
| /ʒ/ televi<u>s</u>ion | /tʃ/ child | /dʒ/ jeans |
| /ŋ/ ri<u>ng</u> | | |

1 Write a word from **B** next to the correct phonetic symbols in **A**.

| A | | B |
|---|---|---|
| 1 /ˈfɑːðə(r)/ | _____ | watch |
| 2 /θɪŋks/ | _____ | just |
| 3 /wɒʃ/ | _____ | father |
| 4 /wɒtʃ/ | _____ | Asian |
| 5 /ˈeɪʒn/ | _____ | thinks |
| 6 /dʒʌst/ | _____ | English |
| 7 /ˈɪŋglɪʃ/ | _____ | wash |

🎧 Listen and check.

2 🎧 Listen. Write the words in the correct box for the <u>underlined</u> sound.

| ~~wea<u>th</u>er~~ | ~~<u>sh</u>op~~ | ~~<u>th</u>irty~~ | dri<u>n</u>k | bro<u>th</u>er |
|---|---|---|---|---|
| <u>th</u>ing | mea<u>s</u>ure | ca<u>tch</u> | revi<u>s</u>ion | tea<u>ch</u>er |
| sta<u>ti</u>on | da<u>ng</u>er | <u>s</u>ure | <u>J</u>anuary | <u>ch</u>ocolate |
| wro<u>ng</u> | | | | |

| /θ/ **thin** |
|---|
| thirty |

| /ð/ **this** |
|---|
| weather |

| /ʃ/ **she** |
|---|
| shop |

| /ʒ/ **decision** |
|---|
| |

| /tʃ/ **chair** |
|---|
| |

| /dʒ/ **fridge** |
|---|
| |

| /ŋ/ **sing** |
|---|
| |

## Vocabulary

### 11 *have* + noun = activity

*have* is often used with a noun to express an action.

> I was **having a bath** when the phone rang.
>
> We **had lunch** in an Italian restaurant.
>
> **Have a good weekend**!

Notice that we don't use *a* with meals.

> I **had breakfast** and went to work.

Complete the sentences with a form of *have* and a noun from the box.

| | | | | |
|---|---|---|---|---|
| an argument | a̶ ̶l̶o̶o̶k̶ | a dream | a swim | a word |
| a shower | a break | a good time | a drink | |

1  Can I **have a look** at your holiday photos?

2  'I went to a party last night.'

'Oh! Was it good? _____ you _____?'

3  Can I _____ with you? There's something I need to talk to you about.

4  I couldn't sleep last night. My neighbours _____ , and I could hear every word.

5  Are you thirsty? Would you like to _____ ?

6  I was tired when I got home, so I _____ , washed my hair, and went to bed.

7  It's so hot! I think I'll _____ in the pool before lunch.

8  I'm tired. Can we _____ soon?

9  I _____ about you last night. I dreamt you were my teacher.

## *Just for fun!*

### 12 Verb + adverb

Find the verb and adverb pairs.

> work  wait
> exercise  ~~drive~~
> explain  forget
> shine

> hard  ~~slowly~~
> regularly  completely
> clearly  patiently
> brightly

drive slowly

_____

_____

_____

_____

_____

### 13 Crossword – irregular verbs

Complete the crossword with the Past Simple of the irregular verbs in the clues.

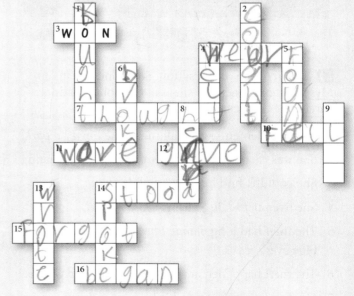

**Across**

3  win (3)
4  find (5)
7  think (7)
10  fall (4)
11  wear (4)
12  give (4)
14  stand (5)
15  forget (6)
16  begin (5)

**Down**

1  buy (6)
2  catch (6)
4  feel (4)
5  drive (5)
6  break (5)
8  hear (5)
9  fly (4)
13  write (5)
14  speak (5)

# 4

Nouns • Expressions of quantity • *something/no one ...*
• Articles • A loaf of bread • Food and clothes
• Pronunciation – diphthongs

**Eat, drink and be merry!**

# Nouns

## 1 High Street shops

Write the shops where you can get these things.

1 a sliced loaf    <u>baker's</u>

2 lamb chops    _____

3 a magazine    _____

4 a holiday brochure _____

5 a book to borrow _____

6 a coat cleaned _____

7 a flat to rent _____

8 a book to buy _____

9 a haircut _____

## 2 Count and uncount nouns

Write the nouns in the correct column.

| apple | sugar | stamp | car | petrol | meat | water | money | dollar | rice |
| job | work | potato | fruit | soup | bread | loaf | news | information | |

| Count nouns | Uncount nouns |
|---|---|
| apple | sugar |
| | |
| | |
| | |

### 3 Chocolate or a chocolate?

1 Sometimes a noun can be countable and uncountable. Look at the pictures and complete the sentences with *a* + noun or just the noun.

1 I like __chocolate__ .

2 Would you like __a chocolate__ ?

3 I drink _coff_ every morning.

4 Can I have _cappu_ ?

5 It's made of _____.

6 It's _____ of juice.

2 Complete the sentences with *some* + noun or *a/an* + noun.

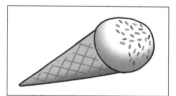

1 I'd like __an ice cream__ , please.

2 Would you like __some ice cream__ ?

3 Can I have _____ ?

4 Have _____ !

5 Can you buy _____?

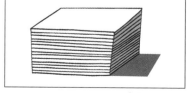

6 I need _____ .

# Expressions of quantity

### 4 some or any?

1 Complete the sentences with *some* or *any*.

1 There isn't _____ milk in the fridge.

2 Is there _____ petrol in the car?

3 Can you buy _____ milk when you go out?

4 I didn't buy _____ grapes.

5 I need to get _____ petrol on my way to work.

6 I need _____ change for the parking meter.

7 I haven't got _____ money.

8 Did you have _____ problems with this exercise?

9 Can you lend me _____ money?

10 Can you give me _____ advice?

2 Correct the mistake in each sentence.

1 Can I have ~~a~~ *some* bread, please?

2 I don't want some rice.

3 I'd like an information about hotels in the town, please.

4 He has done a very good work recently.

5 I haven't got some paper.

6 Can I have any milk in my coffee, please?

### 5 How much? or How many?

Complete the questions with *How much* or *How many*.

1 '_____ children do you have?'
'Three. Two boys and a girl.'

2 '_____ butter do we need?'
'Just one pack.'

3 '_____ eggs did you buy?'
'Half a dozen.'

4 '_____ people are coming for supper?'
'Eight.'

5 '_____ do you earn?'
'That's none of your business!'

6 '_____ bedrooms are there in her house?'
'Three.'

## 6 *much, many,* or *a lot of*?

Look at the picture. Complete the sentences with *much, many,* or *a lot of*.

1  The shop has **a lot of** apples.
2  I can't see **much** bread.
3  There aren't _____ sweets.
4  They haven't got _____ cheese.
5  There are _____ magazines, but there aren't _____ newspapers.
6  There isn't _____ milk.
7  But there are _____ yoghurts.
8  'Is there _____ salt?'   'Yes. Lots!'
9  They don't have _____ butter.
10  There are _____ cans of Cola.
11  There isn't _____ olive oil.
12  There's _____ rice.

## 7 *a few* or *a little*?

Match a question in **A** with a reply in **B** and **C**.

| A | B | C |
|---|---|---|
| 1  'Does your tooth hurt?' <br> 2  'Were there many people at the party?' <br> 3  'Have some cream with your dessert!' <br> 4  'Have you got any books on Russian history?' | 'Just a few.' <br> 'Just a little.' | I'm trying to lose weight.' <br> I'm going to the dentist tomorrow.' <br> You can borrow them if you like.' <br> I didn't know anyone.' |

## 8 Conversation in a shop

Complete the conversation with your own ideas.

**A** Good morning! Can ¹ _____ you?

**B** Yes. I ² _____ grapes, please. ³ _____ they?

**A** £4 a kilo.

**B** ⁴ _____ a nice bunch, please. And ⁵ _____ any bananas?

**A** I'm sorry. I've only got a few left – just three.

**B** OK. Never mind. I need some vegetables. ⁶ _____ any broccoli?

**A** Yes, it's right next to you. Help yourself. ⁷ _____ else?

**B** That's ⁸ _____, thanks. ⁹ _____ is that?

**A** ¹⁰ _____ £3.50, please.

🎧 Listen and compare.

## something/no one …

### 9 Pronouns – *someone* …

Look at the possible combinations.

| some | | one |
|------|---|------|
| any | + | thing |
| no | | where |
| every | | |

**1** Complete the sentences using the words in bold once only.

> **someone     anyone**

1  There's __someone__ on the phone for you.
2  Did __anyone__ ring me last night?

> **everything     nothing**

3  She has _____ – a rich husband and a big house.
4  He has _____ – not a penny to his name.

> **somewhere     everywhere**

5  I can't find my keys! I've looked _____.
6  I want to go away on holiday – _____ hot.

> **anyone     no one**

7  'Who did you speak to at the party?'
   '_____. I just stayed for ten minutes, then I left.'
8  I couldn't see _____ I knew at the party, so I left.

> **someone     everyone**

9  It was a great concert! _____ enjoyed it.
10  Could _____ lend me £5 till the end of the week?

**2** Complete the sentences with one of the words in exercise 1.

1  Does __anyone__ know whose this book is?
2  Please don't worry about me. I'm fine. _____'s the matter.
3  Is there _____ I can do to help with the meal?
4  I'm so unhappy. _____ loves me.
5  I put my glasses _____ safe, and now I can't find them.
6  We're going to sing *Happy Birthday*. _____ has to join in.

## Reading

### 10 Britain's favourite meal – fish and chips

**1** 🎧 Read the introduction and the paragraph *How it all began.* Are the sentences true (✓) or false (✗)? Correct the false sentences.

1  [✗]  The Belgians invented fish and chips.
    **The British invented fish and chips.**
2  [ ]  There are 650 fish and chip shops in Britain.
3  [ ]  Joseph Malin's family fried fish in their home to sell.
4  [ ]  The family lived near a fried fish shop.
5  [ ]  Poor people loved fish and chips because they were delicious and cheap.
6  [ ]  Oliver Twist wrote about fried fish.

**2** Read the rest of the article. Answer the questions.

1  Why do people not believe Joseph Malin's story in the north of England?

_____

2  Why is there a plaque in Mossley market?

_____

3  How many fish and chip shops were there in 1910?

_____

4  How many more shops were there by the 1920s?

_____

5  What outsells fish and chips today?

_____

6  Where are they now fashionable?

_____

**3** Complete the sentences.

1  __The Belgians__ invented chips.
2  _____ was the first person to sell fish and chips in London.
3  _____ wrote about fried fish.
4  _____ sold fish and chips in a market in 1863.
5  _____ opened the biggest fish and chip shop in the world in 1931.
6  _____ serves fish and chips in his restaurant in Paris.

# BRITAIN'S FAVOURITE MEAL — FISH & CHIPS

The Portuguese gave us fried fish. The Belgians invented chips. Then 150 years ago, the British put them together to create fish and chips.

Today Britain has 10,500 fish and chip shops, which earn over £650 million a year. This multi-million pound industry grew from small beginnings.

## How it all began

150 years ago, on the streets of the East End of London, a 13-year-old boy called Joseph Malin had the bright idea of combining fried fish with chips.

Joseph's family were poor, so they began frying chips in a downstairs room of their house to increase the family income. Nearby was a fried fish shop, and Joseph put some fried fish with his chips and walked the streets. He sold the fish and chips from a tray, which hung round his neck. It was a great success. Joseph opened a shop – the first fish and chip shop.

Fish and chips became a favourite with many poor people. They were tasty, cheap, and quick. Charles Dickens, the famous Victorian novelist, wrote about 'fried fish warehouses' in his book *Oliver Twist*.

## The dispute

However, there is a dispute about how the dish began. In the north of England many people don't believe Joseph Malin's story. They say a man called John Lees began selling fish and chips in a market in Mossley, Lancashire in 1863. Today there is a plaque there in his honour.

Whatever the truth, the dish became extremely popular. By 1910 there were more than 25,000 shops across the country and over 35,000 by the 1920s. In 1931 Harry Ramsden from Yorkshire opened a fish and chip 'palace' modelled on the Ritz Hotel in London. It is still the biggest fish and chip shop in the world.

## Fish and chips today

Nowadays other kinds of fast food such as burgers, kebabs, and pizzas all outsell fish and chips. However, in Paris, France, *le fish and chips* is becoming the *chic* new meal. It often appears on menus in fashionable restaurants. 'People love them, for lunch or supper,' says chef Olivier Dupart.

# Listening

## 11  My favourite kind of meal

Listen to four people talking about their favourite meal. Complete the chart.

| | Dave | Sally | Freddie | Lizzie |
|---|---|---|---|---|
| What's his/her favourite meal? | | | | |
| When does he/she have it? | | | | |
| Why does he/she like it? | | | | |
| What's in it? | | | | |

# Articles

## 12 *a*, *the*, or *nothing*?

**1** Complete the sentences with *a/an* or *the*.

1 Pat and Peter are __a__ lovely couple. She has __a__ shop and he's __an__ engineer.

2 We went to ___ cinema to see ___ film about Tolstoy, ___ Russian writer.

3 It was my friend's birthday yesterday. I bought her _a_ bunch of flowers and ___ box of chocolates. She put ___ flowers in ___ lovely glass vase.

4 'Where are ___ children?' 'They're playing in ___ garden.'

5 'Where are my shoes?' 'They're on ___ floor in ___ kitchen.'

6 I'd love to live in ___ house with a balcony near ___ sea.

7 Before you go to bed, can you feed ___ cat and turn off ___ lights?

8 We drove into ___ countryside last weekend and found ___ lovely restaurant next to ___ River Thames. ___ food was excellent.

**2** Match a noun in **A** with a verb in **B** and an ending in **C** to make general statements.

| A | B | C |
|---|---|---|
| 1 Bees | eat | lies. |
| 2 Children | make | honey. |
| 3 Mechanics | play | cars. |
| 4 Politicians | mend | with toys. |
| 5 Butchers | tell | fish. |
| 6 Cats | sell | meat. |

**3** Correct the mistakes in the sentences.

1 I had a lunch with Michael yesterday.

2 Give Maria a ring. She's at the home.

3 I go to the school by bus.

4 My sister's doctor.

5 We have best teacher in world.

6 I usually go to the bed at midnight.

# Vocabulary

## 13 A loaf of bread

Write a word from the box before the nouns. There may be more than one possible answer.

| slice | packet | can | bunch | bottle | piece |
|---|---|---|---|---|---|

1 a __loaf__ of bread
2 a _____ of ham
3 a _____ of beer
4 a _____ of bananas
5 a _____ of crisps
6 a _____ of olive oil
7 a _____ of paper
8 a _____ of Coke
9 a _____ of grapes
10 a _____ of frozen peas
11 a _____ of chewing gum
12 a _____ of flowers
13 a _____ of cake
14 a _____ of biscuits

## 14 Food

Write the words in the correct box. There are five words for each box.

| chicken | lemon | melon | turkey | ham |
|---|---|---|---|---|
| courgette | beef | pea | carrot | onion |
| peach | raspberry | lamb | plum | cauliflower |

| Vegetables | Fruit | Meat |
|---|---|---|
| | | chicken |

# Pronunciation

## 15 Diphthongs

Look at the phonetic symbols for diphthongs (two vowel sounds together).

| | | | |
|---|---|---|---|
| /eɪ/ *name* | /əʊ/ *no* | /aɪ/ *my* | /aʊ/ *how* |
| /ɔɪ/ *boy* | /ɪə/ *hear* | /eə/ *where* | /ʊə/ *tour* |

**1** Write a word from **B** next to the phonetic symbols in **A**.

| A | | B |
|---|---|---|
| 1 /steɪk/ | steak | pie |
| 2 /kəʊk/ | _____ | toy |
| 3 /paɪ/ | _____ | pear |
| 4 /kaʊ/ | _____ | steak |
| 5 /tɔɪ/ | _____ | beer |
| 6 /bɪə(r)/ | _____ | Coke |
| 7 /peə/ | _____ | more |
| 8 /mɔː(r)/ | _____ | cow |

🎧 Listen and check.

**2** Which words rhyme? Match a word in **A** with a word in **B**.

| A | | B | |
|---|---|---|---|
| 1 steak | a | ☐ | sign |
| 2 phone | b | ☐ | boil |
| 3 wine | c | ☑ 1 | cake |
| 4 loud | d | ☐ | here |
| 5 oil | e | ☐ | crowd |
| 6 near | f | ☐ | grown |
| 7 hair | g | ☐ | sure |
| 8 poor | h | ☐ | care |

🎧 Listen and check.

**3** 🎧 Listen and practise saying the sentences.

1 I'd like a rare steak, please.

2 Can I have four ripe pears?

3 Five more beers, a white wine, and a Coke, please.

4 A slice of white bread goes well with mild cheese.

5 I like the same meal every day – olive oil, potatoes, and soy sauce.

## *Just for fun!*

### 16 Word pairs

Find the pairs of words.

eggs  ~~knives~~  butter  chips  ~~forks~~  tie
shirt  fish  salt  bacon  pepper
bread

| knives | and | forks |
|---|---|---|
| | and | |
| | and | |
| | and | |
| | and | |
| | and | |

### 17 Crossword – plural nouns

Complete the crossword. The answers are all plural nouns that end in –s.

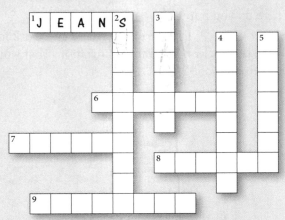

**Across**

**1** Trousers made of denim, usually blue. (5)

**6** The things that you wear, such as shirts, trousers etc. (7)

**7** Steps built between two levels in a building. (6)

**8** Short trousers that end above the knee. (6)

**9** A suit consists of a jacket and ... (8)

**Down**

**2** Glasses to protect your eyes from the sun. (10)

**3** A piece of women's clothing that covers the feet and legs up to the waist. (6)

**4** You use these to cut paper. (8)

**5** You wear these in bed. (7)

# 5

Verb patterns • *I like* and *I'd like* • Future forms
• Pronunciation – confusing vowel sounds • Phrasal verbs

**Looking forward**

## Verb patterns

### 1 Young and old

Read the interviews with Toby and Matilda.
Write the verbs in the correct form.

I   Toby, what would you like [1] **to be** (be) when you grow up?

T   I'd like [2] _____ (work) in space research.

I   Wow! Why do you want [3] _____ (do) that?

T   Well, I enjoy [4] _____ (learn) about the planets, and I love [5] _____ (think) about what's out there in space.

I   Where do you hope [6] _____ (work)?

T   I'd love [7] _____ (go) to Switzerland and work for CERN, the nuclear research organization. That would be my dream job!

I   Well, good luck!

Toby Atkins, nuclear scientist to be

Matilda Jackson, soon to retire

I   Matilda, what are you going to do when you retire?

M   Well, I'm very interested in [8] _____ (find) out about my family history. I've started [9] _____ (do) some research on the net. I'm hoping [10] _____ (find) some cousins who emigrated to Australia.

I   Would you like [11] _____ (go) to Australia?

M   Yes, I would! Australia's a fascinating country. I love [12] _____ (travel)! I've just come back from [13] _____ (drive) across America.

I   Where are you going next?

M   My friend and I are planning [14] _____ (cross) Russia by train. It takes about a week.

I   Wow! That sounds wonderful!

## 2 Hope and ambitions

Write a sentence about each of these people's ambitions.

1 Jane / hope / be / vet / because / love / work / with animals

**Jane hopes to be a vet because she loves working with animals.**

2 Sheila / want / be / teacher / because / enjoy / work / with children

_____

3 Mike / would like / be / farmer / because / like / work / outside

_____

4 James / going to / work / in IT / because / want / earn / a lot of money

_____

5 Jerry / want / be / accountant / because / like / work / with numbers

_____

6 We / think of / buy / a cottage by the sea / because / love / sail

_____

## 3 Infinitive or *-ing*?

Complete the sentences with the infinitive or the *–ing* form. Sometimes both are possible.

1 I need **to get** (get) a job.

2 I hope _____ (earn) a lot of money.

3 I started _____ (learn) English two years ago.

4 We decided _____ (buy) a VW Golf.

5 I stopped _____ (learn) the piano when I was six.

6 She enjoys _____ (visit) new countries.

7 I'm thinking of _____ (go) travelling for a year.

8 I'm fed up with _____ (do) the same thing every day.

9 I'm looking forward to _____ (stop) work.

10 We're trying _____ (save) money for a new house.

## *I like* and *I'd like*

### 4 Questions

<u>Underline</u> the correct question.

1 A <u>Would you like a drink?</u>
  Do you like a drink?

  B Yes, please! I'm so thirsty!

2 A Do you like your teacher?
  Would you like your teacher?

  B Yes, she's really nice!

3 A Do you like going to the cinema?
  Would you like to go to the cinema?

  B Yes, I go every week.

4 A Would you like to go for a swim?
  Do you like going swimming?

  B Yes, that's a good idea. It's so hot today!

5 A Would you like to go out tonight?
  Do you like going out in the evening?

  B Yes, let's go out for a nice meal.

### 5 *would like* or *like*?

Complete the sentences using *would like* or *like* and the verb in brackets.

1 'What sort of books **do** you **like reading** (read)?'
  'Biographies and thrillers.'

2 'Pete told me you've got a new car.'
  'Yes, it's in the garage. _____ you _____ (see) it?'

3 'Why do you have so many cook books?'
  'Because I _____ (cook), of course!'

4 'I'm so cold!'
  '_____ you _____ (borrow) a jumper?'

5 '_____ you _____ (watch) horror films?'
  'Yes, I love the really scary ones!'

# Future forms

## 6 *will* for future facts

Complete the sentences with the phrases in the box.

| 'll see | 'll be | won't take | won't be | won't recognize | 'll soon feel |
|---|---|---|---|---|---|

1 I'm going to have my hair cut short. You _____ me next time you see me.

2 On my next birthday I _____ 30. That's so old!

3 Could you help me carry this box upstairs? It _____ long.

4 Take two of these pills a day and you _____ better.

5 'The film starts at 7.30. I'll see you outside at 7.00.'

   'Don't worry! I _____ late!'

6 Bye! Have a nice evening! I _____ you tomorrow!

## 7 *will* for offers and decisions

Look at the pictures. What are the people saying?
Complete the sentences using *will*.

1 Go and sit down.
   **I'll do** the washing up.

2 It's my turn.
   _____ for this.

3 Don't worry.
   _____ for you.

4 It's ok. _____ it.
   I think it's for me.

## 8 *What's going to happen?*

Look at the pictures. What's going to happen? Make sentences with *going to*.

1 **They're going to run a marathon.**

2 _____

3 _____

4 _____

5 _____

6 _____

## 9 Present Continuous for future arrangements

Put the verbs into the Present Continuous.

1 ' _Are_ you _going_ (go) out tonight?'
  'Yes. I _'m meeting_ (meet) Alan in the pub.'

2 I _____ (have) a party next Saturday.
  Would you like to come?

3 'When _____ we _____ (have) lunch?
  I'm starving!'
  'We _____ (eat) in 15 minutes. Be patient!'

4 'We're all excited because we _____ (go) to
  the zoo tomorrow.'

5 'When _____ you _____ (see) Peter again?'
  'I _____ (have) coffee with him tomorrow.'

## 10 will, going to or the Present Continuous?

Complete the conversations. (Circle) the
correct answer.

1 'Dad! Can you mend my phone for me?'
  'Don't ask me! Ask your brother! ___ it for you.'
  **(a)** He'll do    **b** He's going to do

2 'Why are you buying so much food?'
  'Because some friends ___ for dinner.'
  **a** will come    **b** are coming

3 'Where ___ on holiday next summer?'
  'Turkey. I can't wait!'
  **a** will you go    **b** are you going

4 'What ___ Jill for her birthday?'
  'A big box of chocolates.'
  **a** are you going to buy    **b** will you buy

5 'Oh no, I haven't got enough money to get home.'
  'Don't worry. ___ you some – here's £2.50.'
  **a** I'm lending    **b** I'll lend

6 'Why do you have an appointment with your
  bank manager?'
  'Because ___ my own business, and I need a loan.'
  **a** I'm going to start    **b** I'll start

## Pronunciation

## 11 Confusing vowel sounds

Some words are easy to confuse because the vowel sounds are similar.
Look at these words.

/wəʊnt/ won't    /wɒnt/ want
/wɜːk/ work    /wɔːk/ walk

work    walk

1 🎧 Listen and repeat.

| | | | | | |
|---|---|---|---|---|---|
| 1 | won't | want | 5 | fill | feel |
| 2 | work | walk | 6 | can | can't |
| 3 | chip | cheap | 7 | full | fell |
| 4 | live | leave | 8 | hurt | hit |

2 🎧 Listen and complete the sentences with one of the
words in exercise 1.

1 How do you **feel** today?

2 I _____ a drink.

3 Can I have a _____?

4 Would you like to go for a _____?

5 Don't ask him. He _____ help you.

6 It's a very _____ restaurant.

7 The music's very loud. I _____ hear you.

8 I need to _____ the car with petrol.

9 Where do you _____?

10 Please don't _____ me!

11 I _____ in a cottage near the sea.

12 I _____ down the stairs.

13 I _____ my head.

14 I _____ my leg.

15 My suitcase is _____ .

16 I _____ speak Portuguese very well.

## Reading

### 12 The refugee from Afghanistan

1 🎧 Read the article about Mohammad Razai quickly. Complete the sentences with words from the text.

1 When Mohammad arrived in England, he had _nothing_ .

2 He's studying _____ now.

3 He left Afghanistan because life was _____ for his family.

4 He worked _____ and _____ a lot of exams.

5 He studied biology at _____ .

6 Mohammad is now a British _____ .

7 He wants to be a _____ .

8 He's going to work for the _____ .

2 Read the article again. (Circle) the correct answer.

1 Mohammad travelled to England with his ___ .
  **a** mother      **b** cousin

2 He left Afghanistan when he was a ___ .
  **a** small boy      **b** teenager

3 He ___ where he was going when he left.
  **a** knew      **b** didn't know

4 People in England were very ___ to him.
  **a** cruel      **b** kind

5 ___ encouraged him to take an exam.
  **a** His foster family      **b** A maths teacher

6 He hopes ___ his mother soon.
  **a** to see      **b** to visit

7 Mohammad is going to ___ the UK after he graduates.
  **a** leave      **b** stay in

8 He wants people to understand ___ to leave your own country.
  **a** how hard it is      **b** how easy it is

# The refugee from Afghanistan

**Ten years ago, a boy called Mohammad Razai arrived in England with nothing but a few clothes. Today he is studying medicine at Cambridge University.**

Aged just 15, Mohammad set out from his home country of Afghanistan with his cousin. His mother told him to leave his own country when life became very dangerous for the family. 'I was very sad,' he said. 'I didn't know if I would see my mother again.' They got on a plane but had no idea where they were going. Finally, they got to England.

When they arrived Mohammad was very surprised. 'People were so kind to us. We lived with a foster family. The mother made us feel very welcome. I didn't understand how another human being could help a complete stranger.'

He went to an English school, where he met a maths teacher. The teacher lent him a computer and persuaded him to take an IT exam. 'All the other teachers thought it was too soon, but I passed.'

How did he learn so fast? 'I knew I had to succeed, and to succeed I had to work hard.' He passed more exams and went to University College London, where he studied biology. But his dream was to study medicine at Cambridge.

He finally got a place. 'I still can't believe that I am actually studying at Cambridge,' says Mohammad. He hopes that his mother will get a visa and see him graduate later this year.

He became a British citizen two years ago. He says, 'I love this country. I feel part of British society. I will get married and stay here now. I really want to do something useful. I want to show people that asylum seekers are human beings with feelings, ambitions, and dreams, just like everyone else. People don't leave their own country without a good reason. Leaving home, family, and friends and going to the other side of the world is not easy.'

Mohammad's dream now is to become a paediatrician. He is going to work for the International Red Cross and would like to help children. 'If people have the chance to improve their lives, they will do it with all their heart and soul,' he says. 'They just need the opportunity.'

## Listening

### 14 Three teenagers and their ambitions

1  🎧 Listen and make notes in the chart.

| | Frankie Meazza, 17 | Isabel Blair, 18 | James Owen, 17 |
|---|---|---|---|
| **Life in the past** | | | |
| **Life now** | | | |
| **Hopes for the future** | | | |

### 13 The verb *get*

The verb *get* has many different meanings.
Look at these lines from the reading text.
*They <u>got on</u> a plane ...*
*Finally, they <u>got to</u> England.*
*He finally <u>got</u> a place.*
*I will <u>get</u> married ...*

What does *get* mean in these sentences?
Write a word from the box.

| receive | arrive | become | earn |
|---|---|---|---|
| ~~find~~ | leave | arrive home | |

1  He *got* a job in an office.
   *get* = <u>find</u>

2  What did you *get* for your birthday?
   *get* = _____

3  What time does your train *get in*?
   *get in* = _____

4  I can't run as fast as I could when
   I was 20. I'm *getting* old!
   *get* = _____

5  I *get* £2,000 a month.
   *get* = _____

6  You need to *get off* the bus at the
   Town Hall.
   *get off* = _____

7  What time did you *get in* last night?
   I didn't hear you.
   *get in* = _____

2  Complete the questions with Frankie, Isabel or James.
   Then answer the question.

1  Why were **Isabel** 's parents worried?
   **Because she was so lazy.**

2  How old was _____ when his father died?
   _____

3  Why did _____ leave home?
   _____

4  Where is _____ going to stay in Canada?
   _____

5  Why does _____ want to study medicine?
   _____

6  Why does _____ want to join the army?
   _____

🎧 Listen and check.

# Vocabulary

## 15 Phrasal verbs

**1** Complete the sentences with the verbs in the box in the correct form.

> look (x3)   pick   fill   ~~take~~   try   run   give   get

1  **Take** off your coat and come and sit down.
2  Could I _____ on these shoes, please?
3  You need to _____ in this form and sign it at the bottom.
4  My boss is great. I _____ on really well with him.
5  Can you _____ after my cat while I'm on holiday?
6  Don't drop your litter on the floor! _____ it up!
7  I don't know what this word means. I'll _____ it up in the dictionary.
8  We've _____ out of milk. Can you get some at the shops?
9  I'm trying to _____ up smoking – it's really hard!
10  Can you help me _____ for my glasses. I can't find them anywhere!

**2** Complete the sentences with a particle from the box.

> back   away   down (x2)   round   up (x2)   out (x3)

1  Jack! Wake **up** ! There's someone downstairs!
2  Turn _____ that music! It's too loud!
3  I live in London, but I grew _____ in Manchester.
4  I've got a headache. I'm going to lie _____ for a minute.
5  I'm going to take this jumper _____ to the shop. It's too big!
6  What a pretty dress! Turn _____ ! Let me see it from the back.
7  Did you know Tony's going _____ with an Italian girl called Sofia?
8  My sister and I don't speak to each other. We fell _____ years ago about money.
9  There's a car coming. Look _____! It's going to hit you!
10  That's yesterday's newspaper. You can throw it _____ .

# Just for fun!

## 16 Crossword – countries

Complete the crossword with the countries that go with the nationalities in the clues.

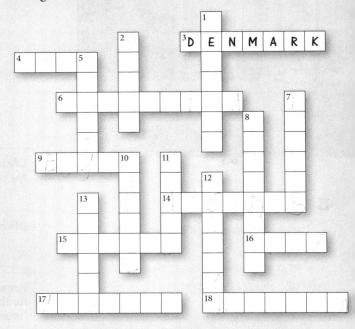

**Across**
**3** Danish (7)
**4** Iranian (4)
**6** Argentinian (9)
**9** Egyptian (5)
**14** Irish (7)
**15** Greek (6)
**16** Iraqi (4)
**17** Dutch (7)
**18** Moroccan (7)

**Down**
**1** Lebanese (7)
**2** Welsh (5)
**5** Norwegian (6)
**7** Polish (6)
**8** Slovak (8)
**10** Turkish (6)
**11** Chilean (5)
**12** Belgian (7)
**13** Israeli (6)

## 17 Capital cities

Complete the sentences with a country.

1  Cairo is the capital of _____ .

2  Buenos Aires is the capital of _____ .

3  Amsterdam is the capital of _____ .

4  Athens is the capital of _____ .

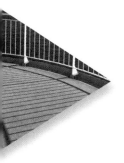

# 6

Describing • *What … like?* • Comparatives and superlatives
• Synonyms and antonyms • Pronunciation – word stress

**The way I see it**

## Describing

### 1 Asking for descriptions

1 Two of the answers to each question are correct. Tick (✓) the correct answers.

1 'How's Jackie?'

a ☐ 'She's very pretty. She's got blonde hair.'

b ☐ 'She isn't feeling very well.'

c ☐ 'Not too good. She's got the flu.'

2 'What does Jackie look like?'

a ☐ 'She's tall, slim, and quite pretty.'

b ☐ 'She's really nice. I like her a lot.'

c ☐ 'She's got long blonde hair and blue eyes.'

3 'What's Jackie like?'

a ☐ 'She's very nice – really good fun.'

b ☐ 'She's quiet but very interesting. You'll like her.'

c ☐ 'She likes the cinema and the arts.'

4 'Do you like Jackie?'

a ☐ 'I adore her. I think she's great!'

b ☐ 'Yes, of course! Everybody loves Jackie!'

c ☐ 'I'm not like Jackie at all!'

5 'What does Jackie like?'

a ☐ 'She's very caring and a great listener.'

b ☐ 'She eats most things. She isn't vegetarian.'

c ☐ 'Old movies and dancing.'

Jackie

2 Write questions about Pete.

1 ' **What does Pete look like** ?'

'He's tall, quite good-looking, and he's got brown hair.'

2 '_____?'

'He's really nice. He's an interesting guy.'

3 '_____?'

'Football, of course! And he likes going to the gym.'

4 '_____?'

'He's fine. Really well.'

5 '_____?'

'Yes, I do. He's one of the nicest people I know.'

3 Write **V** if the word *like* is used as a verb.

1 We both like football.   ☑

2 I'm like my brother.   ☐

3 Who does he look like?   ☐

4 What do you like doing?   ☐

5 Are you like your mother?   ☐

6 What music do you like?   ☐

7 What's your teacher like?   ☐

8 Do you like cheese?   ☐

Pete

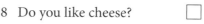

## 2 What ... like?

**1** You have a friend who's living in Australia. Ask questions about the country using *What ... like?*.

1 the weather

   **What's the weather like?**

2 the food

_____

3 the people

_____

4 Sydney

_____

5 the towns

_____

6 the beaches

_____

**2** Match a question in exercise 1 with an answer.

a [3] They're great! Very warm and welcoming.

b ☐ It's really hot in the summer but cooler in the winter.

c ☐ Very tasty! It's a mix of Asian and European.

d ☐ It's a wonderful city. The harbour is beautiful.

e ☐ They're miles long with lovely white sand.

f ☐ They're very modern. Most of them are on the coast.

# Comparatives and superlatives

## 3 big/bigger/biggest

Write the comparative and superlative forms of the adjectives.

|  | Comparative | Superlative |
|---|---|---|
| 1 old | older | the oldest |
| 2 cheap | _____ | _____ |
| 3 big | _____ | _____ |
| 4 fat | _____ | _____ |
| 5 hot | _____ | _____ |
| 6 nice | _____ | _____ |
| 7 safe | _____ | _____ |
| 8 easy | _____ | _____ |
| 9 noisy | _____ | _____ |
| 10 happy | _____ | _____ |
| 11 expensive | _____ | _____ |
| 12 difficult | _____ | _____ |
| 13 intelligent | _____ | _____ |
| 14 modern | _____ | _____ |
| 15 handsome | _____ | _____ |
| 16 good | _____ | _____ |
| 17 bad | _____ | _____ |
| 18 far | _____ | _____ |

big

bigger

biggest

## 4 Comparing two people

Look at the information about Nellie and Matt. Complete the sentences.

| Nellie | | | Matt |
|---|---|---|---|
| **Personal** | | | |
| 30 | 1 | age | 34 |
| ★★ | 2 | clever | ★★★ |
| ★★ | 3 | happy | ★★★★★ |
| **Wealth and job** | | | |
| has $2 million | 4 | money | has $1 million |
| $200,000 | 5 | salary | $150,000 |
| ★★★★★ | 6 | interesting job | ★★ |
| **House** | | | |
| 2000 sq m | 7 | size | 1500 sq m |
| $750,000 | 8 | price | $500,000 |
| 1960 | 9 | date built | 2003 |

1 Nellie is **younger than** Matt.

2 _____ is cleverer than _____ .

3 Matt is a lot _____ than Nellie.

4 _____ is much richer _____ .

5 _____ earns more _____ .

6 Nellie has a much _____ .

7 _____ is bigger _____ .

8 Nellie's house was _____ .

9 Matt's house is _____ modern _____ .

## 5 Superlatives

Write sentences to disagree with these sentences. Use the opposite adjective in its superlative form.

1 I'm the most intelligent student in the class.
   **No, you aren't! You're the most stupid!**

2 She bought the cheapest bag in the shop.
   _____

3 This is the easiest exercise in the book.
   _____

4 I'm the most hard-working student in the class!
   _____

5 James is the meanest person in the world!
   _____

6 Guido's is the best restaurant in town.
   _____

## 6 as … as

Rewrite the sentences using *as … as* or *not as … as*.

1 Your son is already the same height as you!
   Your son is already **as tall as** you!

2 Turkey's hotter than England.
   England isn't _____ Turkey.

3 Her work is good. And my work is good.
   Her work is _____ mine.

4 Jim's taller than me.
   I'm _____ Jim.

5 Jill's more intelligent than Bill.
   Bill isn't _____ Jill.

6 My mother is a better cook than me.
   I can't cook _____ my mother.

## 7 Prepositions

Match a sentence beginning in **A** with a preposition in **B** and an ending in **C**.

| A | B | C |
|---|---|---|
| 1 It's the biggest | as | her brothers. |
| 2 Yours is the same | than | the others. |
| 3 She's older | like | my mother. |
| 4 I look | in | mine. |
| 5 They're different | from | the world. |

## Reading

### 8 Three great things to do in London

1  🎧 Read the article. Complete the sentences with a superlative adjective from the text.

1 The London Eye is _____ tourist attraction in the UK.

2 It is _____ big wheel in Europe.

3 It provides _____ views of the city.

4 The British Museum has _____ collection of ancient artefacts in the world.

5 It is _____ to see the museum over several visits.

6 Regent's Park isn't _____ open space in London.

7 It is _____ formal park.

2 Complete the sentences with a number from the text.

1 The London Eye is _____ metres high.

2 You can see _____ kilometres into the distance.

3 The trip takes _____ minutes.

4 It costs £_____ for an adult and £_____ for a child.

5 The Rosetta Stone was made over _____ years ago.

6 There are over _____ flowers in the rose gardens in Regent's Park.

3 Where does *here* refer to in these sentences?

1 You can hire a boat *here*. _____

2 You can see things from ancient Rome *here*. _____

3 You can see St Paul's Cathedral from *here*. _____

4 You can get married *here*. _____

5 You can see a play *here*. _____

6 You can play games *here*. _____

### Three great things to do in London

**The London Eye**

There are enough things to do in London to fill a lifetime. As the great English writer Samuel Johnson said, 'When a man is tired of London, he is tired of life.' Here are just three suggestions.

**T**he London Eye is the most popular tourist attraction in the UK. It attracts 3.5 million visitors a year.

It's on the south bank of the River Thames. At 135 m, it is the tallest big wheel in Europe, and it provides the best views of the city. You can see the Houses of Parliament and St Paul's Cathedral at your feet, and Windsor Castle to the west, 40 km away.

The wheel rotates at a speed of 26 cm per second (about 0.9 km/h). It doesn't stop to take on passengers, but don't worry – it moves slowly enough to allow people to walk on and off! One trip takes about half an hour. It costs about £16 for an adult and £8.50 for a child. People have parties on it. Some people even get married on it!

**T**he British Museum is situated in Bloomsbury, just north of the centre. It has the biggest collection of ancient Egyptian, Roman and Greek artefacts in the world. Here you can see the Rosetta Stone, made over 2,200 years ago, which provided the key to the understanding of Egyptian hieroglyphs, and the marble friezes from the Parthenon in Greece, known as the Elgin Marbles.

### The British Museum

It is best to see the museum over several visits, rather than trying to see too much at once. The most amazing thing about the museum is that it is FREE!

**R**egent's Park is just to the north of Oxford Street. It isn't London's biggest open space – Hyde Park is – but it is the most beautiful formal park and provides a huge range of attractions. The flower beds are in bloom all year round, and the rose garden (with 30,000 roses!) is filled with colour and perfume in the summer months.

### Regent's Park

There are ponds with ducks, a boating lake, cafés and restaurants, tennis courts, running tracks, and playing fields for football, baseball, and kite flying. There is also London Zoo and the wonderful open-air theatre, which has plays for all ages between May and October. There really is something for everyone!

UNDERGROUND

## Listening

### 9 Visiting London

1 🎧 Listen to an Australian couple who are visiting London for the first time. Look at the pictures, and tick (✓) the places they mention.

St. Paul's Cathedral

The London Eye

Tower Bridge

Madame Tussauds

Buckingham Palace

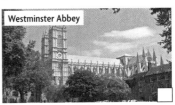
Westminster Abbey

Picadilly Circus

Big Ben

Hyde Park

Trafalgar Square

2 🎧 Listen again. Circle the correct answers.

1 They sat *downstairs / upstairs* on the bus.

2 They began their tour at *Piccadilly Circus / Trafalgar Square*.

3 The Statue of Eros was *smaller / bigger* than they expected.

4 Nelson's Column was *bigger than / as big as* they expected.

5 The Queen *was / wasn't* at home.

6 Big Ben was striking *seven / eleven* when they drove past.

7 Four million people a *month / year* go on the London Eye.

8 Both London and Sydney have a *Hyde / Regent's* Park.

# Vocabulary

## 10 Synonyms and antonyms

**1** Match an adjective in **A** with a synonym in **B**.

| A | B |
|---|---|
| 1 difficult | a ☐ wealthy |
| 2 crazy | b ☐ intelligent |
| 3 rich | c ☐ **1** hard |
| 4 clever | d ☐ huge |
| 5 big | e ☐ mad |

| A | B |
|---|---|
| 6 awful | f ☐ annoyed |
| 7 cold | g ☐ terrible |
| 8 angry | h ☐ good-looking |
| 9 handsome | i ☐ freezing |
| 10 lovely | j ☐ wonderful |

**2** Complete the conversations with a synonym from exercise 1.

1 'This exercise is really hard.'
'I know. It's too **difficult** for me.'

2 'Tony's such a handsome young man.'
'I wish I was as _____ as him!'

3 'The weather's awful today!'
'It's _____! We can't go to the beach.'

4 'Tom is so intelligent!'
'Yes, he's very _____, but he isn't very nice.'

5 'The Empire State Building is big, isn't it?'
'It's _____!'

6 'Why are you so angry with me?'
'I'm _____ that you didn't call me last night.'

**3** Write the antonym of the adjectives using the prefix *un-*, *im-*, or *in-*.

| Adjective | Antonym with a prefix |
|---|---|
| 1 tidy | <u>untidy</u> |
| 2 polite | _____ |
| 3 expensive | _____ |
| 4 happy | _____ |
| 5 interesting | _____ |
| 6 correct | _____ |
| 7 intelligent | _____ |
| 8 possible | _____ |

**4** Complete the chart with the words in the box.

| cheap | wrong | messy | ~~rude~~ |
|---|---|---|---|
| kind | miserable | boring | stupid |

| Adjective | Antonym with another word |
|---|---|
| 1 polite | <u>rude</u> |
| 2 tidy | _____ |
| 3 expensive | _____ |
| 4 happy | _____ |
| 5 interesting | _____ |
| 6 correct | _____ |
| 7 intelligent | _____ |
| 8 selfish | _____ |

**5** Complete the sentences with a word from exercise 4.

1 London is so expensive! Nothing is _____!

2 You're so messy! Why can't you keep your room _____?

3 Pete thought the film was interesting, but I thought it was _____.

4 I thought my answer was wrong, but the teacher said it was _____.

5 My parents are very different. My father is really selfish, but my mother is very _____.

6 I was so happy yesterday, but today I'm totally _____!

7 My brother's teachers say he's intelligent, but I think he's _____.

8 Why are you so rude? It's much easier to be _____.

# Pronunciation

## 11 Word stress

**1** 🎧 Listen to the word stress of the words in the box. Write them in the correct box.

| | | |
|---|---|---|
| ~~beautiful~~ | ~~Japanese~~ | ~~romantic~~ |
| ambitious | interesting | expensive |
| magazine | difficult | sociable |
| wonderful | afternoon | successful |
| apartment | surprising | customer |
| religious | understand | important |
| delicious | yesterday | Mexican |

● ● ●

beautiful

● ● ●

romantic

● ● ●

Japanese

**2** 🎧 Listen and practise saying the sentences.

1 We had a delicious meal in a Japanese restaurant.
2 Jennifer didn't understand the religious ceremony.
3 Christopher has a beautiful apartment in America.
4 The president of Portugal is a very important person.
5 Jonathan is a successful businessman in Switzerland.
6 Patricia is a journalist for a Mexican magazine.

# Just for fun!

## 12 Signs

Where can you see these signs? Write a–f.

1 [a] in a supermarket    4 [ ] on a busy road
2 [ ] in a restaurant    5 [ ] in a shop window
3 [ ] on a cash machine    6 [ ] in an airport

a   Hand baskets only

b   ! DO NOT LEAVE LUGGAGE UNATTENDED

c   ROAD WORKS AHEAD

d   Summer sale! Everything half price

e   No table service

f   Please wait Your cash will follow shortly

## 13 Adjectives

Write the adjectives in the correct column.

~~historic~~ grey **purple** brown **foggy**
~~white~~ **cosy**
~~honest~~ windy **exciting** shy **modern** **orange**
wet lazy sunny cheerful
kind **crowded** **selfish** ~~showery~~ ~~touristy~~
warm black

| People | Places |
|---|---|
| honest | |
| **Colours** | **The weather** |
| | |

# 7

Present Perfect • Present Perfect and Past Simple
• Present Perfect + adverbs • Tense revision
• Pronunciation – sentence stress • Word endings

**Always and ever**

## Present Perfect

### 1 Positive

**1** Complete the text with the verbs in the box in the Present Perfect.

| travel | play | ~~work~~ | be | live | have | meet | climb | cross | see | write | win |
| --- | --- | --- | --- | --- | --- | --- | --- | --- | --- | --- | --- |

## James Macintyre
### *Journalist and traveller*

James Macintyre is 60 years old and as active as ever. He's a journalist, and he ¹ **'s worked** for the *New York Daily* for 22 years. He ² _____ widely in Africa, China, and the Middle East. As a foreign correspondent he ³ _____ many famous world leaders, including Bill Clinton and Nelson Mandela. He's a friend of the US President – they ⁴ _____ golf together on many occasions, and James has always won!

His passion is travel. He ⁵ _____ Mount Kilimanjaro in Tanzania, he ⁶ _____ the Sahara Desert on a camel, and he ⁷ _____ the Northern Lights in Iceland. He ⁸ _____ a number of books about his travels, and he ⁹ _____ several prizes. His story of a train journey between Berlin and Beijing, *Alone Again*, won an award in 2006.

He ¹⁰ _____ married to Alice Bowers, the artist, for 40 years. They have two sons. For the past 15 years they ¹¹ _____ in a beach house on Long Island, New York. 'This is the best place we've ever lived,' says James. 'We ¹² _____ a wonderful life. We're very lucky.'

**2** Complete James' sentences.

1 I **'ve worked** for the same newspaper for over 20 years.

2 I _____ a lot in Africa.

3 I _____ never _____ a game of golf against the US President.

4 I _____ married for 40 years.

5 I _____ in a house on the beach for 15 years.

## 2 Questions and negatives

**1** Look at James' answers. Complete the questions.

1 'How long _____ you _____ for the *New York Daily?*'
'For 22 years.'

2 'Which famous people _____ you _____?'
'Bill Clinton and Nelson Mandela.'

3 '_____ you ever _____ golf with the US President?'
'Yes, I have – many times. I always win.'

4 'How many books _____ you _____?'
'Four. They're all about places I've been to.'

5 'How long _____ you _____ married to Alice?'
'40 years.'

**2** Complete the negative sentences.

1 He/not change jobs for over 20 years

**He hasn't changed jobs for over 20 years.**

2 The US President/not beat him at golf

_____

3 He and his wife/not move house for a long time

_____

4 He/not live in a better place than Long Island

_____

**3** Write the short answers.

1 'Has he been to China?'
' **Yes, he has.** '

2 'Has the US President beaten him at golf?'
' _____ '

3 'Have he and Alice lived on Long Island for a long time?'
' _____ '

4 'Have they ever lived in a better place?'
' _____ '

5 'Has he had a good life?'
' _____ '

## 3 Past Participles

Complete the chart with the Past Simple and the Past participle of the verbs.

| Verb | Past Simple | Past participle |
|---|---|---|
| 1 meet | met | met |
| 2 see | saw | saw |
| 3 write | wrote | written |
| 4 win | _____ | _____ |
| 5 come | _____ | _____ |
| 6 go | _____ | _____ |
| 7 be | _____ | _____ |
| 8 have | _____ | _____ |
| 9 read | _____ | _____ |
| 10 do | _____ | _____ |
| 11 begin | _____ | _____ |
| 12 find | _____ | _____ |
| 13 eat | _____ | _____ |

## 4 *for*, *since*, and *ago*

**1** Complete the sentences with *for* or *since*.

1 I haven't spoken to Harry _____ months.

2 Pete's been in America _____ January.

3 Where have you been? I haven't seen you _____ ages!

4 I've been on holiday _____ a couple of weeks.

5 I've worked in the bank _____ I was 22.

**2** Circle the correct answer.

1 I've been a student of English ___ three years.
   **a** since     **b** for

2 I ___ Peter for a long time.
   **a** 've known     **b** know

3 We haven't seen each other ___ .
   **a** ten years ago     **b** since we were at school

4 I've had a headache ___ Monday.
   **a** for     **b** since

5 I was a waiter ___ ten months. Now I'm a chef.
   **a** for     **b** since

6 I met my wife ___ .
   **a** ten years ago     **b** since ten years

# Present Perfect and Past Simple

## 5 Time expressions

**1** Rewrite the sentences using the Past Simple and the time expression in brackets.

1 I've seen that film. (yesterday)
   **I saw** it **yesterday.**

2 We've arrived in Moscow. (at six o'clock)
   We _____ here _____ .

3 She's bought a new bag. (last week)
   She _____ it _____ .

4 Harry's written a book. (two years ago)
   He _____ it _____ .

5 They've been to Australia. (in 2008)
   They _____ there _____ .

6 She's started her new job. (on 17 July)
   She _____ it _____ .

7 I've lost my phone. (last night)
   I _____ it _____ .

8 Paul's worked as a waiter. (for two months)
   He _____ as a waiter _____ .

9 I've lived in Rome. (when I was a student)
   I _____ there _____ .

10 We've had dinner. (before we left home)
   We _____ a curry _____ .

**2** Write the time expressions from exercise 1 that we use with the Past Simple.

| Past Simple time expressions |  |
| --- | --- |
| *I did it …* | |
| yesterday | _____ |
| _____ | _____ |
| _____ | _____ |
| _____ | _____ |
| _____ | _____ |

## 6 Choosing the correct tense

Put the verbs into the correct tense, Past Simple or Present Perfect.

1 **A** Pete, [1] _____ you ever _____ (live) on your own?
   **B** Yes. When I was studying in Paris, I [2] _____ (have) my own apartment. Why?
   **A** Well, I'm going to university next year, and I'm a bit worried. I [3] _____ never _____ (live) away from home before. I [4] _____ even _____ (not cook) a meal for myself!
   **B** Don't worry! You'll learn.
   **A** [5] _____ you _____ (like) it?
   **B** Yes, I loved it!

2 **A** Hey, Beth! I like your phone!
   **B** Thanks.
   **A** How long [1] _____ you _____ (have) it? I [2] _____ (not see) it before.
   **B** I [3] _____ (have) it for weeks!
   **A** Where [4] _____ you _____ (get) it?
   **B** From the new shop in the High Street.
   **A** How much [5] _____ you _____ (pay) for it?
   **B** Nothing! It was an upgrade!

3 **A** Barney, do you know James Kelly?
   **B** Yes, I [1] _____ (know) him for years.
   **A** Oh! When [2] _____ you _____ (meet) him?
   **B** I [3] _____ (meet) him at a conference in 2006. Then he [4] _____ (go) to America for a couple of years, but he's back in England now.
   **A** What does he do?
   **B** He works for IBM. He [5] _____ (work) for them since he came back from the States.

## Present Perfect + adverbs

**7** *never, already, just, yet*

Put *never, already, just* or *yet* in the correct place in **B**'s lines.

1 **A** You look awful! What's the matter?

   **B** I've just had the most terrible news!

2 **A** Would you like to see that new film at the cinema?

   **B** No, thanks. I've seen it.

3 **A** Where's my white T-shirt?

   **B** I haven't washed it. Sorry.

4 **A** Istanbul's amazing, isn't it?

   **B** I don't know. I've been there.

5 **A** Are there any letters for me?

   **B** The postman hasn't been. He doesn't come till later.

6 **A** Don't forget to phone Tony about Saturday.

   **B** I've spoken to him. He knows all about it.

## 8 Conversations

Complete the conversations using the verbs in the box in the Present Perfect.

| ~~meet~~ read have eat try take |
|---|

1 'What's your new boss like?'

   'I don't know. I **haven't met** her yet.'

2 'Are you hungry?'

   'Yes, I'm starving! I _____ anything yet today!'

3 'What do you think of that book I lent you?'

   'I'll tell you later. I _____ it yet.'

4 'Do you like Thai food?'

   'I've no idea. I _____ never _____ it.'

5 'Would you like a cup of coffee?'

   'No, thanks. I _____ already _____ two cups.'

6 'Mmm! That cake looks good! Can I have some?'

   'Not yet. I _____ only just _____ it out of the oven.'

## Tense revision

**9** Present, Past or Present Perfect?

Complete the sentences about the singer, Joe Ford. Circle the correct answer.

| **PROFILE** | |
|---|---|
| **Joe Ford** | |
| City | Manchester |
| School | Manchester Grammar School 1993–2000 |
| Wife | Vicky, journalist at *The Guardian*, met at school |
| Band | Soul Boys |
| Biggest hit | *Never ever* (2008) |

1 Joe Ford ___ with his wife in Manchester.

   **a** has lived    **b** lived    **c** lives

2 He ___ to Manchester Grammar School.

   **a** has gone    **b** goes    **c** went

3 His wife, Vicky, ___ for *The Guardian* newspaper.

   **a** writes    **b** wrote    **c** has written

4 He and his wife ___ each other since school.

   **a** known    **b** have known    **c** knew

5 Joe ___ in a band called Soul Boys.

   **a** sings    **b** has sung    **c** sang

6 They ___ a number 1 hit with their song *Never ever* in 2008.

   **a** had    **b** have had    **c** have

# Reading

## 10 14,000 miles on a 'pizza delivery bike'

**1** 🎧 Read the article about Simon Gandolfi's journey quickly. Answer the questions.

1  How old is Simon?  __He's 76 years old.__

2  Is he married? _____

3  What kind of motorbike did he ride?

_____

4  Where did his journey start and end?

_____

5  How long did it take? _____

6  Where is he going next? _____

**2** Read the text again more carefully. Correct the information in these sentences.

1  Simon is ~~very~~ <sup>a little</sup> overweight.

2  He hasn't ridden a motorbike for 50 years.

3  The journey was 4,700 miles long.

4  He was kidnapped for five weeks in Chile.

5  He broke his arm in Chile.

6  He paid $18 for a hotel room in Bolivia.

7  He hopes to be in England for his 77th birthday.

8  He's never been to India.

# 14,000 miles on a 'pizza delivery bike'

19142928

**Simon Gandolfi** is 76 years old and lives in Herefordshire, England. He's a little overweight, has a bad back, and has had two heart attacks. Despite all this, he has just ridden the length of America on a 'pizza delivery motorbike'. Simon's wife, Bernadette, and their two sons couldn't believe it, but he wanted to prove to them that he could do it.

He began his journey in Veracruz on the Gulf of Mexico, and it was there he bought a Honda 125cc – the original pizza delivery bike. He says: 'I chose a Honda 125cc because I could buy it new in Mexico for just £1,200, and it does 120 miles to the gallon.'

> What I've done is no big deal. If I can do it, anyone can.

He last rode a motorbike 40 years ago, and at first he was terrified by all the traffic on the city freeway. Fortunately, he met a kind police officer who suggested a suitable route.

The 14,000 mile journey took Simon from Mexico through South America and then north, finishing in Pennsylvania, USA. He rode at a height of 4,700m in Bolivia and through the Amazon jungle, he was kidnapped for a short time in Venezuela, and spent five weeks in a hotel in Chile with a broken leg after falling off his bike on an icy road. He mostly slept in small family hotels. The price of rooms varied from country to country: US$18 in Veracruz, half that in Bolivia.

The journey took six months, and everyone he met and talked to on the way treated him with kindness. He says: 'What I've done is no big deal. If I can do it, anyone can. I love travelling and meeting new people.'

> Last time I went I was young and ignorant.

Next month he is going to India for six months, again by motorbike. He hopes to celebrate his 77th birthday in Goa. He says: 'It's been 40 years since I was last in India, and I want to see not only what has changed there, but how I have changed. Last time I went I was young and ignorant.'

# Listening

## 11 Till death us do part

1 🎧 Listen to the interviews with Ethel and Norman Reiss and Shirley Meldon. Who says these lines? Write **E & N** (Ethel and Norman) or **S** (Shirley).

1 'We've been married for 50 years.'       **E & N**

2 'We were married for 48 years.'       _____

3 'We never had an argument about anything.'       _____

4 'Sure we have arguments! But then we say sorry.'       _____

5 '… we've lived in the same area all our married life.'       _____

6 'We lived in a cottage near the sea.'       _____

7 '… he was the only man I ever loved.'       _____

8 '… he's the only man I've ever loved.'       _____

2 🎧 Listen again to the interview with Ethel and Norman. Complete the sentences.

1 'Time _____.'

2 '_____ best friends …'

3 'Do you ever _____ ? '

4 'Tell me … where _____?'

5 'No, we've _____ here.'

3 🎧 Listen again to the interview with Shirley. Complete the sentences.

1 'Bruce _____ ago. I _____ own now for two years.'

2 'We _____ when we were _____.'

3 'You keep _____. Don't give in! Every marriage has _____.'

4 '_____ you and Bruce _____ arguments?'

5 'I _____ flat in a small town.'

# Pronunciation

## 12 Sentence stress

Look at the extract from the interview with Ethel and Norman. Notice the sentence stress.

🎧 Listen line by line and repeat. Then read the whole extract aloud.

**I** Tell me … where did you two meet?

**N** We met at a dance, on a Saturday night …

**E** I saw this good-looking boy on the other side of the room …

**N** Oh, I saw her as soon as she walked in. It took me a while to ask her to dance …

**E** We started going out together, and two years later we got married.

**I** And … where did you live?

**E** We bought a tiny cottage in a village, and we've lived in the same area all our married life.

**I** Wow! So you've never moved away?

**N** No, we've always lived around here.

**E** He's the only boyfriend I've ever had, and he's the only man I've ever loved.

**N** You daft old thing!

# Vocabulary

## 13 Word endings

**1** Complete the chart. <u>Underline</u> the stressed syllable.

| Noun | Person | Adjective |
|------|--------|-----------|
| 1 <u>hi</u>story | <u>histor</u>ian | <u>histor</u>ical |
| 2 <u>poli</u>tics | _____ | _____ |
| 3 <u>art</u> | _____ | _____ |
| 4 <u>mu</u>sic | _____ | _____ |
| 5 <u>che</u>mistry | _____ | _____ |
| 6 <u>sci</u>ence | _____ | _____ |
| 7 eco<u>no</u>mics | _____ | _____ |
| 8 pho<u>to</u>graphy | _____ | _____ |

**2** Complete the sentences with a word from exercise 1.

1 Van Gogh didn't show any **<u>artistic</u>** talent until he started painting in his twenties.

2 When water turns into steam, there is a _____ reaction.

3 Marie Curie was a Polish _____, famous for her work on radioactivity.

4 Mozart showed great _____ talent from an early age.

5 Margaret Thatcher was a British _____ .

6 The _____ of *homo sapiens* began in Africa about 80,000 years ago.

7 The world is experiencing serious _____ problems at the moment.

8 The first _____ image was produced in 1826 by the French inventor Joseph Nicéphore Niépce.

**3** Complete the chart.

| Noun | Adjective |
|------|-----------|
| 1 **fame** | famous |
| 2 ambition | _____ |
| 3 _____ | successful |
| 4 _____ | healthy |
| 5 fashion | _____ |
| 6 _____ | noisy |
| 7 comfort | _____ |
| 8 _____ | popular |

## Just for fun!

## 14 Crossword – people

Complete the crossword.

### Across

2 A doctor for animals. (3)
5 The children of your aunt and uncle. (7)
7 Someone who works in the legal profession. (6)
8 The prime _____ is the leader of the government in countries such as Britain. (8)
10 A woman whose husband has died. (5)
11 Someone who owns a farm. (6)
13 Someone who comes from another country. (9)
15 Members of your family who lived a long time before you. (9)
17 Someone who is travelling in a car, plane, train or boat but is not the driver. (9)

### Down

1 Someone who has to leave their country because of danger. (7)
3 Someone who steals something. (5)
4 Someone who works in politics. (10)
6 Someone who is in an army. (7)
9 Someone who comes to live in a country. (9)
12 Someone who uses violence for political reasons. (9)
14 Someone who shows people around a place, for example a town or museum, and gives them information about it. (5)
16 Someone who likes somebody or something, for example a pop star or football team, very much. (3)

# 8

*have to* • *should* • *must* • Verb + noun
• Pronunciation – sounds and spelling

**Girls and boys**

## have to

### 1 Positive, negative, question

1 Complete the interview with professional football player, Tony Mancini, using the lines in the box.

| | | | | |
|---|---|---|---|---|
| have to play | has to be | do you have to run | ~~have to be~~ | have to watch |
| do you have to do | has to run | don't have to go | doesn't have to watch | |

**Tony Mancini**

**I** Tony, what do you need to do to be a successful footballer?

**T** Well, professional footballers [1] **have to be** very fit. Sometimes we [2] _____ two matches a week.

**I** What [3] _____ to keep fit?

**T** I go to the training ground most days.

**I** What kind of training do you do?

**T** Well, at 10.00 on Monday mornings we start with a run.

**I** How far [4] _____?

**T** About five miles! That wakes you up on a Monday, I can tell you!

**I** Does everybody do that?

**T** Oh, yes! Well, actually, the captain [5] _____ further than anyone else!

**I** Why?

**T** It's a bit of a joke! Because he's the leader, he [6] _____ the best! On other days we do circuit training or match practice.

**I** Do you train every day?

**T** No. Just four days a week. Wednesday is usually a free day, so I [7] _____ to the ground that day.

**I** What do you do on your day off?

**T** My wife and I usually do something together – shopping, lunch or just a walk. Then in the afternoon, I often play golf.

**I** Do you have a special diet?

**T** I [8] _____ what I eat very carefully – lots of carbohydrates, such as pasta and rice, and low-fat meat.

**I** Your matches are usually at the weekends. Does your wife watch?

**T** Yes, she does. She [9] _____, but she says she enjoys it.

2 Complete the questions using *have to*.

1 'What time **does** Tony **have to** start training on Monday morning?'
'10 o'clock.'

2 'How many miles _____ the players _____ run?'
'Five.'

3 'How many days a week _____ Tony _____ train?'
'Four.'

4 'What sort of food _____ footballers _____ eat?'
'Lots of carbohydrates and low-fat meat.'

5 '_____ Tony's wife _____ watch him play?'
'No, she doesn't. But she likes to.'

## 2 Possession and obligation

Does *have* mean possession (**P**) or obligation (**0**) in these sentences? Write **P** or **0**.

1  He has a really good job.                                    P

2  She has to work really hard.                               0

3  How many hours a day does she have to work?    ____

4  Does he have a lot of meetings?                          ____

5  I have a lot of homework tonight.                        ____

6  I have to do it before tomorrow.                         ____

7  How many exercises do we have to do?              ____

8  When can we have a coffee break?                     ____

## 3 Past – *had to/didn't have to*

Complete the lines in the conversation between Beth and her grandmother with a form of *have to*.

**B** Grandma, when you were a child, [1] _____ you _____ do any housework?'

**G** Of course! I [2] _____ help my mother in the kitchen!

**B** And [3] _____ your brother _____ help, too?

**G** Yes. He [4] _____ work on the farm with my father.

**B** What about school? [5] _____ children _____ do homework back then?

**G** Yes, we did. Lots!

**B** And [6] _____ you _____ take lots of horrible exams like me?

**G** No, we [7] _____ do as many exams in those days. Maybe life was better then, after all!

## 4 Me and my family

Write ten true sentences about you and your family, using the chart.

| I | | do the washing-up. |
|---|---|---|
| We | | do the ironing. |
| My parents | | do the shopping. |
| My mother | have to | go to work. |
| My father | has to | get up early. |
| My brother | doesn't have to | go to school. |
| My sister | don't have to | do homework. |
| My grandmother | | do housework. |
| My grandfather | | pay tax. |

1  __My grandfather doesn't have to go to work.__

2  _____

3  _____

4  _____

5  _____

6  _____

7  _____

8  _____

9  _____

10  _____

## 5 Correcting mistakes

Correct the mistake in each sentence.

   *doesn't have*

1  He ~~hasn't~~ to work. He's a millionaire.

2  Have you to wear a uniform in your job?

3  I have study very hard because I want to get a good job.

4  We not have to get up early tomorrow. It's Saturday!

5  When I was a child I have to help my mother with the housework.

6  Do you have to an English lesson today?

# *should*

## 6 Advice

1 Give advice to these people. Use *I think … should …* or
*I don't think … should …* and a phrase from the box.

| | | |
|---|---|---|
| eat so much cake | ~~go to work~~ | feed her |
| go by bus instead | get married | go to the dentist |
| take them back to the shop | | |

1 Mary's got a bad cold.
**I don't think she should go to work.**

2 Tony wants to drive to work, but he hasn't got his glasses.
_____

3 My tooth hurts.
_____

4 James and Amy are only 16, but they want to get married.
_____

5 The baby's crying. I think she's hungry.
_____

6 I'm so fat! My trousers don't fit me anymore!
_____

7 There's a hole in my shoe. I only bought them last weekend.
_____

2 Ask for advice in these situations. Use *Do you think …
should …?*

1 Tom has asked me to marry him.
**Do you think I should say yes?**

2 We want to go somewhere hot for our holiday.
Where _____ ?

3 I can't decide whether to get a job or go to university.
What _____ ?

4 We're going to have a party at our flat, but it's so small!
How many people _____ ?

5 Dave's parents are coming for dinner.
What _____ ?

## 7 *have to* or *should*?

Complete the sentences with a form of *have to*
or *should*.

1 'Jeff works too hard.'
'I agree. I really think he **should** slow down.'

2 When you're in the army, you _____ do what
you're told.

3 I'm going to bed now. I _____ be up very early.

4 You've got a terrible cough. You really _____
stop smoking.

5 'You haven't met my boyfriend, have you?'
'No. You _____ invite him round for a drink.
I'd love to meet him.'

6 'Tim doesn't want to go to school tomorrow.'
'He _____ go! He has no choice!'

7 I think you _____ get your hair cut. It's getting
very long.

8 '_____ we _____ go to Jenny's party?'
'Yes, we do! She's expecting us.'

9 'My boyfriend expects me to do his washing
for him.'
'I don't think you _____. Tell him to do it
himself.'

10 'I'm going on a driving holiday in England.'
'Remember you _____ drive on the left!'

## must

### 8 Obligation

Complete the sentences with *must* and a verb in the box.

| call | ~~buy~~ | write | go | tidy | meet | look after |
|------|---------|-------|-----|------|------|------------|

1 It's my mother's birthday next week. I **must buy** her a present.

2 My bedroom's such a mess! I _____ it up before anyone sees it.

3 Mary's a lovely girl. You _____ her. You'll love her!

4 I haven't spoken to Sally for ages. I _____ her soon.

5 You can borrow my suit, but you _____ it. It was very expensive.

6 There's a great film on at the cinema. You _____ and see it!

7 There are so many things I need from the shops! I _____ a list or I'll forget them.

### 9 *mustn't* or *don't have to*?

Complete the sentences with *mustn't* or *don't/doesn't have to*.

1 You _____ tell lies. It's very naughty.

2 You _____ come with me if you don't want to.

3 The British Museum is free. You _____ pay.

4 Jimmy is very ill. He _____ get out of bed.

5 Tell your children they _____ pick the flowers in my garden!

6 I have the day off tomorrow, so I _____ get up early.

7 Vanessa is very rich. She _____ go to work.

8 Sh! The baby's asleep! You _____ wake her!

## Reading

### 10 The helicopter pilot

1 🎧 Read about Linda Lewis. Complete the sentences with a word and a number.

1 Linda has worked as a **pilot** for more than __10__ years.

2 She got her _____ after _____ years.

3 You have to fly for at least _____ hours to become a _____ pilot.

4 She worked in Wisconsin for _____ years. She had to transport huge _____ .

5 In her present job she has to work for _____ hours a _____ .

6 She works for _____ days and then has six days _____ .

# The helicopter pilot

**Linda Lewis is from North Carolina in the USA. She has been a helicopter pilot for over ten years.**

Linda has always been interested in jobs usually done by men. At first she wanted to be a firefighter, but after her first flying lesson, that was it, she decided to become a pilot.

> **Linda had to pay for all her lessons.**

It wasn't easy. Maria had to pay for all her flying lessons. She says: 'Most pilots get their training in the military so they don't have to pay for their lessons'. Each lesson cost $150 an hour. It took Linda two years to get her licence. You have to have at least 150 hours of flying to be a commercial pilot so Linda spent more than $30,000 learning to fly. To help pay for her lessons, she sold her car, her skis, and her camera. She also borrowed money from a friend.

When she got her licence Linda spent six years working in logging camps in Wisconsin. She had to carry huge logs from the forest to trucks. Today

**2** Read the text again. Are the sentences true (✓) or false (✗)? Correct the false sentences.

1　✗　Linda always wanted to be a pilot.
　　　**At first she wanted to be a firefighter.**

2　☐　Military pilots have to pay for lessons.

3　☐　A friend lent her some money to pay for lessons.

4　☐　She had to cut down trees in Wisconsin.

5　☐　She now works as a flying doctor.

6　☐　She doesn't have to fly when the weather is very bad.

7　☐　The students at her school come from the US.

8　☐　Last summer she spent some time in Italy.

9　☐　She thinks that there should be more scholarships for military pilots.

she works as a rescue pilot. She carries patients to care centres and hospitals. 'The challenge comes when you have to pick somebody up from a difficult accident spot.' Linda has to work 12 hours a day for six days. She waits in a bunk house with other pilots for a call. 'If the weather's bad, I have to decide if the flight is possible or not.' After six days of work, she has six days off.

> **Today she works as a rescue pilot.**

Linda has also opened a helicopter school for students from all over the world. 'Training students is fun. They are so excited about flying.' She's made friends with a lot of the students. Last summer she spent a week in the villa of a friend near Florence, Italy and went to Rome to a convention for helicopter pilots.

She says: 'It's still hard for women. They have to compete with all the military pilots who have the advantage of excellent training. There should be more scholarships for women pilots.'

# Listening

## 11 The train driver

🎧 Listen to the interview with train driver, Sue Hipperson. Look at the questions she is asked and make notes as you listen.

1　How long have you been a train driver?
_____

2　Do you earn a good salary?
_____

3　What's the best thing about the job?
_____

4　Are there any disadvantages?
_____

5　How did you become a train driver?
_____

6　Do you meet any interesting people?
_____

7　Do you have to wear a uniform?
_____

8　Is it difficult for a woman in what is usually a man's job?
_____

9　What's your advice to young women who are interested in the job?
_____

# Vocabulary

## 12 Verb + noun

**1** Write the words in the box in the correct column.

| ~~friends~~ | the housework | my homework | a cake |
| the shopping | an IT course | a phone call | your best |
| up my mind | the washing-up | me a favour | a noise |

| make | do |
|------|-----|
| friends | |

**2** Complete the sentences with the correct form of a *make* or *do* phrase in exercise 1.

1 Saturday morning is when we __do the housework__ . I do the ironing, and my husband cleans.

2 It's Oliver's birthday tomorrow, so I'm going to _____ . I need 15 candles!

3 I don't know if I want the steak or the fish. I can't _____ .

4 Good luck in your exam. Just _____ . I'm sure you'll pass.

5 Could you _____ ? Can you get me some stamps when you're at the shops?

6 It can be difficult to _____ when you move to a new area. But you soon get to know people.

7 I'm going to the supermarket to _____ . Do you need anything?

8 Do you mind if I _____ ? I need to ring my boss.

**3** Write the words in the box in the correct column.

| a photo | some music on | your glasses on |
| my advice | the date in my diary | a long time |
| suncream on | the children to the zoo | your coat off |

| take | put |
|------|-----|
| | |

**4** Complete the sentences with the correct form of a *take* or *put* phrase in exercise 3.

1 'What are you doing this weekend?' 'I'm _____ . They love animals.'

2 Everyone stand together! I want to _____ .

3 'I can't read this menu.' '_____ ! Then you'll be able to read it!'

4 'Can you come to my party on the 18th?' 'Oh, yes. I'll _____ now.'

5 You must be patient. It _____ to get better after a serious illness.

6 Do you mind if I _____ ? Jazz? Pop?

7 I really think you should _____ and stop smoking.

8 You must _____ when you lie in the sun – factor 20, at least!

# Pronunciation

## 13 Sounds and spelling

**1** 🎧 Listen and ⟨circle⟩ the correct phonetic symbol for the vowel sound on the left.

| | | | | |
|---|---|---|---|---|
| 1 | fr**ie**nd | **a** /ə/ | **b** /e/ | **c** /ɜː/ |
| 2 | l**ea**rn | **a** /ɜː/ | **b** /ɔː/ | **c** /ʌ/ |
| 3 | w**a**r | **a** /æ/ | **b** /ɑː/ | **c** /ɔː/ |
| 4 | g**oo**d | **a** /ʊ/ | **b** /ʌ/ | **c** /uː/ |
| 5 | f**oo**d | **a** /uː/ | **b** /ɔː/ | **c** /ɜː/ |
| 6 | fr**ee** | **a** /ɪ/ | **b** /ɒ/ | **c** /iː/ |
| 7 | k**i**nd | **a** /ɪə/ | **b** /aɪ/ | **c** /ɔɪ/ |
| 8 | c**a**ke | **a** /aɪ/ | **b** /əʊ/ | **c** /eɪ/ |
| 9 | n**ow** | **a** /əʊ/ | **b** /aʊ/ | **c** /ɪə/ |

**2** Match the words that rhyme.

| | | | | |
|---|---|---|---|---|
| 1 | word | a | ☐ | Paul |
| 2 | bread | b | ☐ | June |
| 3 | height | c | 1 | bird |
| 4 | beat | d | ☐ | said |
| 5 | ball | e | ☐ | meet |
| 6 | should | f | ☐ | white |
| 7 | find | g | ☐ | loud |
| 8 | soon | h | ☐ | signed |
| 9 | crowd | i | ☐ | wood |

🎧 Listen and check.

**3** The same vowel sound can have different spellings.
/ɔː/: /fɔː/ *four*  /wɔː/ *war*  /mɔː/ *more*  /lɔː/ *law*

Complete the words.

| | | | |
|---|---|---|---|
| 1 | /ɔː/ | s_____t | f_____th |
| 2 | /ɜː/ | h_____t | w_____ld |
| 3 | /uː/ | fr_____t | thr_____gh |
| 4 | /aɪ/ | m_____ne | h_____ght |
| 5 | /əʊ/ | sl_____w | j_____ke |

🎧 Listen and check.

## *Just for fun!*

## 14 Crossword – clothes

Complete the crossword. The answers are all things you can wear.

```
¹D R E ²S S
```

**Across**
1 A piece of women's clothing that covers the body and part of the legs. (5)
3 A piece of women's clothing that hangs from the waist. (5)
6 You wear this around your waist to keep your clothes in place. (4)
9 A set of clothes, usually a jacket and trousers or skirt. (4)
11 The top half of a suit. (6)
12 A soft hat with a peak that comes out over your eyes. (3)
13 You wear this round your neck when it's cold. (5)
14 Another word for a sweater. (6)
15 You wear these on your feet in warm weather. (7)

**Down**
2 Short trousers that end at or above the knee. (6)
4 A man might wear this with a shirt when he wants to look smart. (3)
5 You wear these on your feet inside your shoes. (5)
6 A type of shoe that covers the foot and part of the leg. (5)
7 You wear these on your hands when it's cold. (6)
8 You wear these in bed. (7)
10 Shoes that you wear to do sports. (8)

## 9

Past Perfect • Joining sentences • Homonyms
• Narrative tenses • Pronunciation – pronunciation of *-ea*

**Time for a story**

## Past Perfect

**1   The Pied Piper of Hamelin**

**1**   Complete the story with the verb forms in the boxes.

| Past Simple | | | | | |
|---|---|---|---|---|---|
| appeared | ran | left | led | ~~ate~~ | drowned |

| Past Perfect | | | | | |
|---|---|---|---|---|---|
| had heard | had been | ~~had come~~ | had eaten | had brought | had done |

# The Pied Piper of Hamelin

**A** long time ago there was a town called Hamelin in Germany. It was a wealthy town, and everyone ¹ **ate** well.

But then there was a plague of rats. No one knew where the rats ² **had come** from. They ³ _____ up and down every street and in and out of every house. Soon the rats ⁴ _____ every scrap of food in the town. No one had any idea how to get rid of them.

One day a stranger ⁵ _____ . He said he was a rat-catcher called the Pied Piper. The people of Hamelin promised to give him as much gold as he wanted if he could get rid of the rats.

The Pied Piper walked along the streets. He ⁶ _____ a special pipe with him, and he played a tune that no one ⁷ _____ before. Rats came out of every corner of the town and followed the Pied Piper. He ⁸ _____ them to the river, where they all ⁹ _____ .

The people of Hamelin were delighted, but it seemed to them that it ¹⁰ _____ very easy for the man to get rid of the rats, so they refused to pay him. The Pied Piper ¹¹ _____ the town in a fury.

A few days later he returned while the townspeople were in church. Once again, he played a tune on his pipe. This time all the children of Hamelin followed him, just as the rats ¹² _____ before. The Pied Piper led the children out of the town and into the mountains, and they were never seen again.

The parents knew it was their fault. Music was never heard again in the streets of Hamelin.

**2** Put the verbs in brackets into the Past Perfect.

1 The people were horrified because there _____ never _____ (be) a plague of rats before.

2 When the Pied Piper arrived in Hamelin, no one _____ (see) him before.

3 He got rid of the rats because the people _____ (promise) to give him a lot of gold.

4 When the townspeople came out of church, the children _____ (disappear).

5 The Pied Piper wanted revenge because the people of Hamelin _____ (not pay) him.

## 2 … because …

**1** Make sentences from the chart.

| A | B | C |
|---|---|---|
| 1 I was hungry | | spent it all on clothes. |
| 2 I was tired | | eaten anything all day. |
| 3 I didn't have any money | because I'd | slept well the night before. |
| 4 I was late for work | because I hadn't | set my alarm clock. |
| 5 My mother was worried | | been in touch for a week. |
| 6 My father was angry | | crashed his car. |

**2** Complete the sentences using the verb once in the Past Simple and once in the Past Perfect.

**had**

1 I was hungry because I **hadn't had** time to eat all day.
2 I was hungry, so I **had** a sandwich and a bowl of soup.

**go**

3 I was tired last night, so I _____ to bed early.
4 I didn't see Jane at the party. She _____ home before I arrived.

**give**

5 I didn't have any money, so Jimmy _____ me £10.
6 Henry was a poor man when he died. He _____ all his money to charity.

## 3 Reordering a story

Look at the pictures. Complete the story using the Past Perfect. Begin at picture 4.

JAMES BOND GOT UP EARLY.

HE FLEW TO THE MEXICAN DESERT.

HE KILLED THE EVIL VILLAIN, PROFESSOR ZAROS.

HE SAVED THE WORLD FROM DESTRUCTION.

*At the end of the day, James Bond sat in his hotel room. He'd had a busy day.* **He'd saved the world from destruction.** _____

_____

_____

_____

# Joining sentences

## 4 Conjunctions

**1** Match a line in **A** with a line in **B**.

| A | B |
|---|---|
| 1  She didn't enjoy the party because | a ☐  I couldn't answer any of the questions. |
| 2  Although he was a millionaire, | b ☐1  she didn't know anybody there. |
| 3  He was tired, so | c ☐  I tried them in America. |
| 4  I didn't like hamburgers until | d ☐  he bought all his clothes second-hand. |
| 5  She was a beautiful woman, but | e ☐  he went to bed. |
| 6  I was so nervous in the interview that | f ☐  she had a terrible temper. |

**2** Join the pairs of sentences using the conjunction. Change one verb into the Past Perfect.

1   **when**

I read the letter. I threw it away.

**When I'd read the letter I threw it away.**

2   **after**

The guests went home. I tidied up.

_____

3   **although**

He earned a lot of money in his life. He died a poor man.

_____

4   **before**

I left the house. She woke up.

_____

5   **until**

We didn't stop cleaning. We did every room in the house.

_____

6   **as soon as**

I wrote my essay. I went to bed.

_____

7   **so**

I was very rude to him. I rang and apologized.

_____

8   **but**

I ran to the station. The train already went.

_____

## 5 Things parents say

Here are some things that parents say to their children. Complete the sentences with a conjunction.

| while  when  but  ~~before~~  or |
|---|
| because  until |

1   Remember to brush your teeth **before** you go to bed.

2   Do what I say _____ I'll send you to your room!

3   _____ someone says 'hello' to you, say 'hello' back.

4   You're laughing, _____ it's not funny.

5   You can't have an ice-cream _____ you didn't eat your vegetables.

6   _____ you're at school, I have to go out to work.

7   You can't leave the table _____ you've eaten what's on your plate.

# Vocabulary

## 6 Homonyms

Some words have more than one meaning.

*I'm reading a good **book**.*

*I'd like to **book** a table at your restaurant.*

Dictionaries give the different meanings.

**book 1** /bʊk/ *noun* [C]  a written work that is published
**2** /bʊk/ *verb* [I, T]  to arrange to have or do something at a particular time

---

**1**  The words in the box have more than one meaning. Check you know them.

| fan   wave   boot   ring   type |
| --- |

**2**  Complete the pairs of lines with a word from exercise 1.

1

Jeremy and I got engaged! Do you like my _____?

Give me a _____ later. We'll have a chat.

2

I'm a big _____ of country and western music.

It's so hot! Could you switch the _____ on?

3
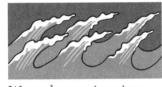

We can't go swimming. The _____ are too big.

Oh, look! There's Bertie! _____ to him!

4

How many words a minute can you _____?

She likes all _____ of dogs.

5

I like your _____! Where did you get them?

You can put your suitcase in the _____.

---

**3**  Complete the pairs of lines with a word from the box.

| fine   play   fair   lie   mean   ~~watch~~   match   flat |
| --- |

1  a  Do you want to **watch** the football at my house?
   b  'What time is it?'  'I don't know. I forgot to put my **watch** on.'

2  a  'How are you?'  '_____, thanks. And you?'
   b  I had to pay a £40 parking _____! I was so annoyed!

3  a  He didn't tell me the truth. He told me a _____!
   b  I've got a headache. I'm going to _____ down.

4  a  He's so _____! He never buys anyone a drink.
   b  I don't understand. What do you _____?

5  a  We saw a _____ by Shakespeare at the theatre last night.
   b  Would you like to _____ chess with me?

6  a  Did you enjoy the football _____ last night?
   b  I need a _____. I want to light these candles.

7  a  Everyone in my family is very _____. We all have blond hair and pale skin.
   b  You gave her £10, but you only gave me £1. That's not _____!

8  a  Do you live in a house or a _____?
   b  Holland is a very _____ country. There are no mountains.

# Listening

## 7 A love story

🎧 Listen to the conversation. Amanda and Peter have just met again after many years. Answer the questions.

1 Does Amanda recognize Peter immediately?

_____

2 Where does Peter work?

_____

3 Why has Peter come back to the town?

_____

4 Why has Amanda come back to the town?

_____

5 Why didn't Peter travel the world?

_____

6 What's his job? Does he enjoy it?

_____

7 What doesn't Amanda do any more?

_____

8 Did Peter leave Amanda or did Amanda leave Peter?

_____

9 Why does Peter think that their relationship ended?

_____

# Reading

## 8 Love story

🎧 Read *Things we never said* – the story of Peter and Amanda. Answer the questions.

### *Things we never said*
#### by Fiona Goble

Peter recognized her immediately. It was 15 years since they had been together, but he still thought about her all the time. She didn't see him at first. She was looking in a shop window.

'Hello, Amanda,' he said softly.

'Peter!' As she said his name memories flooded back. Their first summer together when they were both 18, and they had sat together by the river on a perfect sunny afternoon. He had told her that he couldn't live without her.

'I'm surprised you recognized me,' he said.

'Really?' she smiled. In fact, she often thought about him. 'Have you moved back here?' She knew he hated the town and had wanted to leave and travel the world.

'Good heavens, no,' he said. 'I work in London now. I've come back for my dad's 70th birthday. He's having a huge party.'

'Great! You must be looking forward to it,' she said, although she knew he had never got on with his father.

'Yes,' he said. In fact, he didn't feel a lot for his father, who had treated his mother badly when he was growing up.

'What about your parents?' He asked. 'Are they well?'

'Yes, they're fine,' she said. 'They're excited about

1 How long is it since they last met?

_____

2 How old were they when they first met?

_____

3 What did they do the first summer they were together?

_____

4 Why didn't Peter get on well with his father?

_____

my sister's wedding on Saturday. That's why I'm back in the town.'

'That's nice,' he said, although he remembered that she had never particularly liked her little sister.

'Are you in a hurry?'

'No, not really.'

'Well, let's go for a coffee.'

They walked to the Café Bella on the High Street. They had spent hours here when they had first met.

'So, Peter. Did you travel the world?' she asked.

'Ah, no, I didn't. I studied law instead. I'm a lawyer.'

She looked at his expensive suit, so different from the jeans and T shirt he'd worn as a student.

'Wow! Do you enjoy it?'

'Yes, I do,' he lied. 'And what about you? Do you still paint? I loved your paintings.'

'I haven't painted anything for years. I've just had a few temporary jobs in offices.'

Amanda paused, and then, suddenly, she said, 'Oh Peter, I don't know why I left you that day.'

He looked at her. Then he looked away. 'It's OK. We were very young, too young. It happens. People break up.' He knew how much he had missed her. He knew that he still loved her, but he said nothing.

'Yes, you're right.' She felt hurt because he seemed to have no regrets. 'Well, I must go. I have to help mum with the flowers for the wedding. Goodbye Peter.'

'Bye, Amanda. Nice to see you.'

5 Is Amanda's sister younger or older than her?

_____

6 Where did they go for coffee? Had they been there before?

_____

7 Does Peter enjoy his job?

_____

8 Why did Amanda feel hurt?

_____

## Narrative tenses

**9 Revision**

Complete the sentences about the story with the verb in brackets in the correct form.

1 When Peter and Amanda **met** (meet) in the street, they **hadn't seen** (not see) each other for 15 years.

2 Amanda _____ (look) in a shop window when Peter _____ (speak) to her.

3 When they were 18, they _____ (spend) a lot of time together, and Peter _____ (tell) her that he _____ (love) her.

4 Peter _____ (leave) the town because he _____ (want) to travel the world.

5 He _____ (come) back for his father's 70th birthday party.

6 He _____ (feel) sorry for his mother because his father _____ (treat) her badly.

7 Peter _____ (wear) an expensive suit. When he was a student he _____ (wear) more casual clothes.

8 Peter _____ (miss) Amanda a lot, but he _____ (not say) anything.

9 They _____ (not arrange) to meet again.

# Pronunciation

## 10 Pronunciation of -ea

There are different ways of pronouncing -ea.
Look at the phonetic symbols.

| | | | |
|---|---|---|---|
| /iː/ | meat | /e/ | dead |
| /ɪə/ | dear | /eə/ | wear |
| /eɪ/ | break | /ɜː/ | learn |

**1** 🎧 Listen. Write the words in the correct column.

| heat | earth | team | bread | great | mean |
|---|---|---|---|---|---|
| fear | bear | health | bean | steak | read (past) |
| pear | head | year | earn | read (present) | |

| /iː/ | /e/ | /ɪə/ |
|---|---|---|
| heat | | |

| /eə/ | /eɪ/ | /ɜː/ |
|---|---|---|
| | | |

**2** Look at the pairs of words. Is -ea pronounced the same (✓) or differently (✗)?

| | | | |
|---|---|---|---|
| 1 | ✓ | dear | clear |
| 2 | ✗ | pear | earth |
| 3 | ☐ | health | wealth |
| 4 | ☐ | learn | mean |
| 5 | ☐ | wear | bear |
| 6 | ☐ | great | meat |
| 7 | ☐ | meat | steak |
| 8 | ☐ | break | beard |
| 9 | ☐ | fear | bread |
| 10 | ☐ | dead | head |
| 11 | ☐ | learn | pear |
| 12 | ☐ | year | team |

🎧 Listen and check.

## Just for fun!

### 11 Who arrived first?

What order did people arrive at the party?

When I arrived at the party, Jane and John had just left. They'd had a good chat to Sophie and Pete, who'd been there from the start. Alice had arrived just after they had. Jane and John had arrived ten minutes after Alice, just after Henry arrived. As I was taking off my coat, Sally came in the door. She said that Pat and Paul were on their way, but they'd been caught in the traffic. In fact, they didn't get there till midnight, when everyone else was leaving.

1  <u>Sophie and Pete</u>
2  _____
3  _____
4  _____
5  _____
6  _____
7  _____

### 12 Crossword – opposite verbs

Complete the crossword with the opposite of the verbs in the clues.

**Across**
2 take off (a plane) (4)
4 break (4)
6 pull (4)
8 lend (6)
10 win (4)
11 start (6)
12 throw (5)
14 forget (8)

**Down**
1 open (5)
3 export (6)
5 pick up (4)
7 spend (money) (4)
9 shout (7)
10 arrive (5)
11 pass (an exam) (4)
13 laugh (3)

# 10

Passives • Compound nouns • Pronunciation – silent letters

**Our interactive world**

# Passives

## 1 Tenses and infinitives

**1** Complete the newspaper articles using the passive verb forms in the boxes.

| were developed | has been developed | will be used | be produced | are used |
| --- | --- | --- | --- | --- |

**1** **Scientists develop mobile phone battery that can be charged in just ten seconds**

A revolutionary mobile phone battery that recharges in ten seconds instead of several hours [1] _____ by scientists. This is 100 times faster than existing batteries.

The invention is based on the sort of lithium batteries that [2] _____ in most laptops, digital cameras, iPods, and phones. These batteries store a large amount of energy in a small space.

The new batteries [3] _____ by engineers at the Massachusetts Institute of Technology.

The MIT team say their invention uses materials that are freely available, and it could [4] _____ in large quantities very easily.

In the next few years, it [5] _____ in all kinds of portable gadgets. The same technology could also be used for producing batteries for electric cars.

| was hit | will be closed | was killed | were injured | were taken |
| --- | --- | --- | --- | --- |

**2** **25 injured in motorway pile-up**

Twenty-five people [1] _____ in an accident on the M40 motorway yesterday afternoon. Five of the injured [2] _____ to hospital by helicopter. Fortunately, no one [3] _____ .

The accident happened between junctions 11 and 12 at five o'clock as motorists were driving home. A car braked sharply and [4] _____ by the car behind. This caused a multiple pile-up involving fifteen cars, three lorries, and a van.

The motorway is still blocked, and [5] _____ until this afternoon.

**2** Complete the questions. (Circle) the correct answer, **a** or **b**.

**1** 'What sort of batteries ____ in laptops and cameras?'
  **a** use    **b** are used
  'Lithium batteries.'

**2** 'Who ____ the new battery?'
  **a** developed    **b** was developed
  'Engineers at the Massachusetts Institute of Technology.'

**3** 'How many people ____ in the motorway accident?'
  **a** injured    **b** were injured
  '25.'

**4** 'What ____ the accident?'
  **a** was caused    **b** caused
  'A car braked sharply and was hit by the car behind.'

## 2 Forming the passive

Put the verbs in brackets into the correct passive tense.

**Present Simple**

1 70% of the earth's surface _is covered_ (cover) by water.
2 My car _____ (insure) against accidents and theft.
3 We _____ (watch) by CCTV cameras everywhere we go.
4 What time _____ the post _____ (deliver)?
5 You _____ (cover) in paint! What have you been doing?
6 A lot of information about our lives _____ (keep) on computer.
7 Every year about 2,000 people _____ (kill) in road accidents in the UK.

**Past Simple**

1 We _weren't affected_ (not affect) by the flood, but our neighbours were.
2 _____ your car _____ (damage) in the accident?
3 The painting _____ (sell) for ten million dollars.
4 I _____ (introduce) to a very interesting man at the party yesterday.
5 The door _____ (lock) so I couldn't open it.
6 Where were you when these photos _____ (take)?

**Present Perfect**

1 All these problems _have been discussed_ (discuss) many times before.
2 _____ you ever _____ (question) by the police?
3 I _____ (sack) from my job! What did I do wrong?
4 Our plane _____ (delay) because of bad weather.
5 Brian's doing well at work. _____ just _____ (promote) to area manager.

**_Will_**

1 You _'ll be told_ (tell) what to do when you arrive.
2 Your exam results _____ (send) in the post.
3 Where _____ the next Olympic Games _____ (hold)?

## 3 Questions

Put the words in the correct order to make questions. Then choose the correct answer from the box.

> In China.      More than 100 million!
> In India.      ~~Flour, yeast, and water.~~
> Between 60 and 80 million people.

1 bread/made/is/from/What/?
  ' _What is bread made from?_ '
  ' _Flour, yeast and water._ '

2 Hindi/spoken/Where/is/?
  ' _____ '
  ' _____ '

3 people/killed/How many/in the Second World War/were/?
  ' _____ '
  ' _____ '

4 held/Where/the Olympic games/were/in 2008/?
  ' _____ '
  ' _____ '

5 iPhones/made/How many/been/have/?
  ' _____ '
  ' _____ '

## 4 Short answers

Correct the information in these sentences.

1 Paper is made from plastic.
  _No it isn't! It's made from wood._
2 Champagne is made in Scotland.
  _____
3 iPhones are made by Nokia.
  _____
4 The *Mona Lisa* was painted by Van Gogh.
  _____
5 The Pyramids were built in Greece.
  _____

## 5 The passive infinitive

Complete the sentences with the passive infinitive of the verbs in the box.

| clean | serve | ~~do~~ | spend | knock down |
|-------|-------|--------|-------|------------|
| cancel | take | contact | ban | |

1 The situation is serious. Something must **be done** immediately.

2 More money should _____ on health care.

3 Please go and sit at the table. Dinner will _____ in five minutes.

4 Can you take my suit to the dry cleaner's? It needs to _____ before the wedding.

5 Smoking should _____ in public places.

6 These pills must _____ with food twice a day.

7 The old factory is going to _____ tomorrow.

8 The football match had to _____ because of bad weather.

9 I'm not taking my phone, so I can't _____ while I'm away.

## 6 Active or passive?

1 Choose the best way to follow the sentences. (Circle) **a** or **b**.

1 I live in an old house. …
   a Someone built it 200 years ago.
   b It was built 200 years ago.

2 She wears the most beautiful clothes. …
   a They're all made in Italy.
   b People in Italy make them all.

3 I bought some shoes, but I never wore them …
   a so I sold them on eBay.
   b so they were sold on eBay.

4 Do you like this painting? …
   a It was done by me.
   b I did it myself.

5 The *Mona Lisa* is the most famous painting in the world. …
   a It can be seen in the Louvre in Paris.
   b People can see it in the Louvre in Paris.

6 We all have breakfast together every morning. …
   a Then the children are taken to school by me.
   b Then I take the children to school.

2 Read about the inventor, Trevor Baylis. Put the verbs in brackets into the correct tense, active or passive.

# Trevor Baylis
## Inventor of the clockwork radio

Trevor Baylis [1] _____ (grow up) in London. He [2] _____ (educate) at a local school and then [3] _____ (study) engineering at a technical college in the city.

He is best-known for the invention of the world's first clockwork radio, in 1991. He wanted to produce a radio that could [4] _____ (use) by people in parts of Africa where there wasn't any electricity to get information about health and AIDS.

No manufacturer wanted to produce his early attempts, but then, in 1994, his radio [5] _____ (show) on a TV programme. A South African businessman [6] _____ (invest) money in the project, and the first clockwork radios, called *Freeplay*, [7] _____ (manufacture) in South Africa in 1995. Since then the radios have been a great success, and millions [8] _____ (sell) around the world.

Over the years Trevor Baylis [9] _____ (give) many awards for his invention. He continues to work hard. In 2003, he [10] _____ (start) a company which aims to help new inventors get financial backing. The company [11] _____ (base) in Richmond, London, where the famous inventor lives.

# Reading

## 7 Look who we found on the Internet!

**1** 🎧 Read the article. Complete the sentences about the people's relationship to each other.

1 Charlotte is _Guy's wife, Zoe and Will's mother, and Rose's stepmother._

2 Fred was _____ .

3 Guy is _____ .

4 Zoe is Charlotte's _____ .

5 Will is Charlotte's _____ .

6 Rose is Guy's _____ .

**2** Write the correct name. Who's …?

1 a widow _____    3 a stepsister _____

2 divorced _____    4 dead _____

**3** Read the article again. Answer the questions.

1 How did Fred die?
_____

2 What kind of business did Charlotte start?
_____

3 What did she call the Internet dating site?
_____

4 What kind of daddy did the children want?
_____

5 Did Charlotte email Guy immediately?
_____

6 Why did Rose want her dad to meet Charlotte?
_____

7 What else was found on the Internet?
_____

8 Who designed the wedding invitation? What was it like?
_____

# Look who we found on the Internet!

**W**hen **Charlotte Morgan's** husband, **Fred**, was killed in an aircrash, she was left to bring up their two small children alone. Charlotte was heartbroken but determined to be strong for her children. She started a successful photographic business, and she also surprised her kids by learning to ride powerful motorbikes.

But by the time daughter **Zoe** was 11 and son **Will** was 9, what they really wanted was a new dad. Will said: 'We need a new daddy. What are you going to do about it?' Charlotte, 41, had already searched Internet dating sites but with no success. So she handed her laptop to her two children, showed them a website, and said, 'This is a 'daddy shop'. You choose one.'

The children searched through the photos. They wanted a daddy with a 'nice smile' and 'kind eyes'. Finally, they found **Guy Bolam**, a 44-year-old divorced father with one daughter. They called their mother to the screen. Charlotte looked at the photograph. All she could see was a motorbike. 'It's him, the man on the bike,' the children said.

Charlotte told them 'no', and she continued looking for different people, but each time she showed the kids someone, they just said, 'No, man on a bike.'

Eventually, Charlotte sent Guy an email and attached a photo. Guy showed it to his daughter, **Rose**. She said, 'I couldn't tell much from the picture, but I knew dad wasn't happy being alone.'

Guy invited Charlotte on a first date, and they got on well immediately. Nine months later Guy asked Zoe, Will, and Rose for permission to ask Charlotte to marry him. A short time later he texted them: 'She said yes!' The engagement ring was also found on the Internet, and Rose helped her father choose it.

The wedding invitation was designed by all three children. The story of how Charlotte and Guy met was written on the front in Zoe's handwriting. It reads:

'Where they met (on the Internet)! They had a first date. They fell in love! They met the kids, Guy proposed. Married!!!'

Sometimes it can be as simple as that. They now all live happily together in an old farmhouse in Essex. Charlotte says, 'I feel very, very lucky indeed.'

# Listening

## 8 Internet dating disasters

**1**  Listen to four stories about Internet dating disasters. Answer the questions.

### Cathy's story: Too good to be true
Posted on April 15th
1 What was the only good thing about Cathy's date?
2 What did they talk about?
3 What lies did he tell?

### Michelle's story: Nightmare meeting
Posted on March 23rd
4 Who did Michelle take with her on the date?
5 What was her date wearing?
6 Why did she leave so hurriedly?

### Adrian's story: It wasn't in the stars
Posted on November 1
7 Who did his date want to talk about?
8 Why did they not meet again?
9 Who did she finally date?

### Shona's story: Mr Ego
Posted on May 14th
10 What couldn't Shona find on the Internet?
11 How old was her date?
12 Who did he talk about?

**2** Whose date says these lines? Write **C** (Cathy), **M** (Michelle), **A** (Adrian), or **S** (Shona).

1 'Darling, I'm so sorry. I had a meeting with my publisher.' ____

2 '… I'm a Scorpio and you're a Gemini. It won't work.' ____

3 'It's the best. It's real 'cowboy' food.' ____

4 'I've got something to show you. Look at these.' ____

5 'Go, go, go!' ____

6 'Aren't my kids the cutest?' ____

7 'You weren't nearly as boring as I thought you would be.' ____

 Listen again and check.

**3** Why is …

1 Cathy's date 'too good to be true'? _____

2 Michelle's date 'a nightmare meeting'? _____

3 Adrian's story called 'it wasn't in the stars'? _____

4 Shona's story called 'Mr Ego'? _____

## 9 Past participles as adjectives

Many past participles can be used as adjectives. Circle the correct adjective.

1 She was *heartbroken* / *determined* when her husband left her for another woman.

2 Tom worked really hard. He was *annoyed* / *determined* to do well in his exams.

3 We were *amused* / *shocked* to learn that Paul's in hospital. What's the matter with him?

4 I hope I get the job. I'll be so *disappointed* / *amused* if I don't.

5 I was really *delighted* / *surprised* to see Pete at work today. I thought he was ill.

6 My dad was *amused* / *horrified* when he saw my latest tattoo. He hates it!

7 My new computer is behaving strangely again. I'm really *annoyed* / *delighted*.

8 I didn't laugh out loud at the play, but I was quite *amused* / *talented*.

9 Their son is so *disappointed* / *talented*. He can play the cello and piano really well.

10 I love Anne's parties. I was *horrified* / *delighted* when I got the invitation.

# Vocabulary

## 10 Compound nouns

**1** Write a word to make three compound nouns.

1 post / business / fire → **man**

2 _____ → ache / lights / phones

3 pop / rock / film → _____

4 _____ → break / beans / shop

5 return / parking / single → _____

6 _____ → cut / brush / dresser

7 petrol / railway / bus → _____

8 _____ → set / glasses / cream

9 cook / address / note → _____

10 _____ → lights / warden / jam

**2** Write a compound noun from exercise 1.

1 **petrol station**

2 _____

3 _____

4 _____

5 _____

6 _____

7 _____

8 _____

**3** Answer the questions using a compound noun.

1 When do people take aspirin? **for a headache**

2 If you want a recipe, where do you look? _____

3 Who delivers the post to your house? _____

4 If you park in the wrong place, what might you get? _____

5 What should you put on your skin before you sunbathe? _____

6 What can you watch at the end of the day? _____

7 What must you switch on when you are driving at night? _____

8 Where can you buy petrol? _____

# Pronunciation

## 11 Silent letters

1 🎧 There are many silent letters in English words. Listen and repeat the words.

/raɪt/ ~~w~~rite   /tɔːk/ ta~~l~~k   /ˈaʊə(r)/ ~~h~~our   /ˈɑːnsə(r)/ ans~~w~~er

2 Cross out the silent letters in the words.

1 ~~k~~now

2 listen

3 climb

4 island

5 foreign

6 farm

7 walk

8 wrong

9 autumn

10 could

11 sandwich

12 daughter

🎧 Listen and check. Practise saying the words.

3 Look at the phonetic spelling of these words from exercise 1. Write the word.

1 /wɔːk/     __walk__

2 /faːm/     _____

3 /ˈaɪlənd/     _____

4 /kʊd/     _____

5 /klaɪm/     _____

6 /ɔːtəm/     _____

7 /ˈfɒrɪʒn/     _____

8 /ˈlɪsn/     _____

9 /ˈsænwɪdʒ/     _____

🎧 Listen and check. Practise saying the words.

## Just for fun!

### 12 Crossword – the High Street

Complete the crossword.

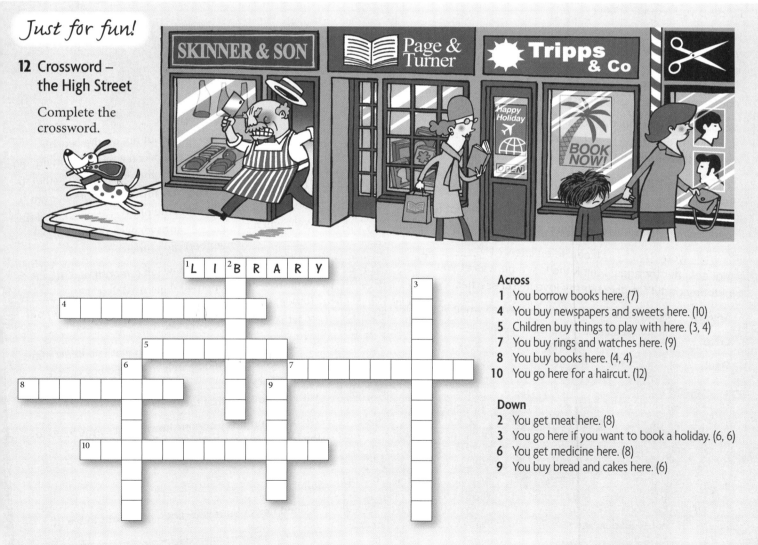

**Across**

1 You borrow books here. (7)
4 You buy newspapers and sweets here. (10)
5 Children buy things to play with here. (3, 4)
7 You buy rings and watches here. (9)
8 You buy books here. (4, 4)
10 You go here for a haircut. (12)

**Down**

2 You get meat here. (8)
3 You go here if you want to book a holiday. (6, 6)
6 You get medicine here. (8)
9 You buy bread and cakes here. (6)

# 11

Present Perfect Simple and Continuous • Tense review
• Phrasal verbs • Pronunciation – words that sound the same

**Life's what you make it**

## Present Perfect Simple

### 1 Two emails

Complete the emails with the verbs in brackets in the Present Perfect Simple or Past Simple.

**1**

Hi Sally

I ¹ _____ (not hear) from you for a while, so I thought I'd drop you a quick email.

How are you? ² _____ you _____ (start) your new job yet? The last time we ³ _____ (speak) a month or so ago you had just heard that you'd got the job, but you ⁴ _____ (not know) when you had to start. I hope your old company ⁵ _____ (give) you a big party when you left!

You usually go on holiday to Greece at this time of year, so maybe you ⁶ _____ (go) away already. You could be reading this email on the beach!

I'm fine. My only news is that I ⁷ _____ (buy) a new flat, which I'm moving into in a few weeks' time. I ⁸ _____ (find) it on the Internet, and it's perfect for me – near where I work and top floor, so there's plenty of light.

⁹ _____ you _____ (see) Helen lately? I ¹⁰ _____ (not see) her for ages! I think the last time was at your birthday party! Do give her my love if you see her.

Anyway, I hope you're OK. Send me an email when you can.

Love

Paul

**2**

Dear Paul

You're right. I'm in Greece but not on the beach! I ¹ _____ (be) here for just over a week, and I'm having a wonderful time. ² _____ you ever _____ (be) to Greece? If you haven't, you must come – it's heaven on earth! I come to the same place every year, and this year when I ³ _____ (arrive) even the taxi driver ⁴ _____ (remember) my name!

I ⁵ _____ (start) my new job a month ago. It's all very new, but I suppose I'll get used to it. I ⁶ _____ (made) some new friends, and we ⁷ _____ (be) out together a few times. It's OK.

I ⁸ _____ (not see) Helen either, but I do know some of her news! She's madly in love! With a boy called Rafael. They ⁹ _____ (know) each other for a year without realizing that they were soul mates!

Well, the sun has just gone down, so it's time to go to the bar for a drink. I'll raise my glass to you!

Lots of love

Sally

PS Good news about your flat – can't wait to see it!

## 2 Questions

Complete the questions about the emails on page 74.

1 'When _____ Paul last _____ (speak) to Sally?'
  'A month or so ago.'

2 'What _____ he just _____ (buy)?'
  'A new flat.'

3 'Where _____ he _____ (find) it?'
  'On the Internet.'

4 'When _____ he last _____ (see) Helen?'
  'At Sally's birthday party.'

5 'How long _____ Sally _____ (be) in Greece?'
  'Just over a week.'

6 '_____ she _____ (start) her new job yet?'
  'Yes, she has.'

7 '_____ she _____ (see) Helen recently?'
  'No, she hasn't.'

8 'How long _____ Helen and Rafael _____ (know) each other?'
  'For a year.'

## 3 *been* or *gone*?

Complete the conversations with *been* or *gone*.

1 'Can I speak to Jack?'
  'Sorry. He's on holiday. He's _____ to Spain.'

2 'Look at your suntan! Have you _____ on holiday?'
  'Yes, we've _____ to Spain.'

3 'Where's Tony?'
  'He's _____ to school. He'll be back this afternoon.'

4 'Why is there no one in the office?'
  'They've all _____ home. It's after six o'clock.'

5 'Have you ever _____ to Russia?'
  'No, I haven't. What's it like?'

6 'Hi, Suzy! I'm back. Is everything OK?'
  'No! Where have you _____? We have so much work to do!'

# Present Perfect Continuous

## 4 Forming the tense

Complete the sentences with the verbs in the box in the Present Perfect Continuous.

| look   play   watch   try   learn   study   revise   ~~work~~ |

1 Joe and Stephanie **have been working** really hard to save money to buy a house.

2 Tony and James _____ tennis for hours! They must be exhausted!

3 Alice _____ medicine for three years, and she still has three more years to do before she graduates.

4 I _____ Spanish because my girlfriend's from Madrid, and we're going to see her family next month.

5 We _____ for a flat to rent for months, but it's impossible to find something we can afford.

6 I _____ to get hold of my sister for days, but she isn't answering her phone.

7 Sorry I missed your call. I _____ television, and I didn't hear my phone.

8 Dan's so tired! He _____ for his exams all weekend, and now he's exhausted!

## 5 Forming the question

Complete the questions. Put the verbs in brackets into the Present Perfect Continuous.

1 Sorry I'm late. _____ you _____ (wait) long?

2 How long _____ you _____ (play) chess? You're very good!

3 The streets are wet! _____ it _____ (rain)?

4 What _____ the children _____ (do)? They're filthy!

5 How long _____ he _____ (go out) with Ann?

6 _____ you _____ (watch) the new series on TV? It's great!

## 6 What's she been doing?

Match a line in **A** with a line in **B**.

| A | B |
|---|---|
| 1 Ann's been sunbathing. | a ☐ We've got dirty fingernails. |
| 2 She's been shopping. | b ☐ She's crying. |
| 3 We've been gardening. | c ☑ She's a bit burnt. |
| 4 She's been watching a sad film. | d ☐ The whole house is clean! |
| 5 I've been waiting for hours! | e ☐ I can smell garlic. |
| 6 He's been doing the housework. | f ☐ She has ten new pairs of shoes. |
| 7 She's been cooking. | g ☐ They're all sweaty! |
| 8 They've been jogging. | h ☐ I'm absolutely furious with you! |

## 7 Present Perfect Simple or Continuous?

Choose the correct form of the verb. (Circle) the correct answer.

1 'Why are you all wet?'
   'Because I ___.'
   **(a)** 've been swimming     **b** 've swum

2 'Aaatchoo!'
   'Oh dear! That sounds like a bad cold. How long ___ it?'
   **a** have you had     **b** have you been having

3 'Jerry and Sophie make a lovely couple.'
   'It's true. How long ___ together?'
   **a** have they gone out     **b** have they been going out

4 'What have you had to eat today?'
   'I ___ two hamburgers, a banana, and two ice-creams.'
   **a** 've had     **b** 've been having

5 'What was that noise?'
   'It was Jack. He ___ your favourite vase!'
   **a** 's broken     **b** 's been breaking

6 'Wow! You play guitar really well!'
   'Thanks. I ___ lessons for a few months.'
   **a** 've had     **b** 've been having

7 'Kate! Hi! How are you?'
   'Pete! How lovely to see you! What ___ for the past few months?'
   **a** have you done     **b** have you been doing

8 'Have you finished your homework yet?'
   'Yes. I ___ my essay, so I'm going to bed now.'
   **a** 've finished     **b** 've been finishing

# Tense review

## 8 Present and past

Put the verbs in brackets into the correct tense, Present or Past Simple, Present Perfect Simple or Continuous.

1 I [1] _____ (learn) Italian for the past three years. My teacher is very good, and I [2] _____ (like) her very much.
   I [3] _____ (be) to Italy three times. I [4] _____ (go) there last year with my family, and we [5] _____ (stay) in Florence. I [6] _____ never _____ (see) anywhere more beautiful than Florence in my whole life! We [7] _____ (spend) three days going round the museums.

2 My daughter [1] _____ (try) to find a job for months. She [2] _____ (leave) university in June, and since then she [3] _____ (have) one or two part-time jobs. She [4] _____ (work) in a café for the last two weeks.

   She [5] _____ (want) to work in publishing. She [6] _____ (write) dozens of letters of application, and she [7] _____ (have) a few interviews but no job offers yet.

## 9 All tenses

Read the magazine interview with the actress, Juliette Binoche.
Put the verbs in brackets into the correct tense. Choose from the tenses in the box.

| Present Simple | Present Continuous | Past Simple | Past Continuous | Present Perfect Simple | Present Perfect Continuous |

# The 60 second interview

## Juliette Binoche

Juliette Binoche was born in Paris. She is an actress and also a passionate painter. She is involved in politics and fund-raising for charities. She has two children, a boy and a girl.

**How long have you been in the acting profession?**
I [1] _'ve been acting_ (act) since I was a teenager.

**Where did you learn to act?**
I [2] _____ (train) at the National Conservatory of Dramatic Arts in Paris.

**How many films [3] _____ you _____ (make)?**
Over 40.

**[4] _____ you ever _____ (win) any awards?**
Yes, I won an Oscar in 1997 for my role in a film called _The English Patient_. There have been other awards, too.

**What [5] _____ your parents _____ (do) when they were younger?**
My father was a director, and my mother was an actress. They [6] _____ (get) divorced when I was four.

**What is your earliest memory?**
I was two. I fell over and banged my head as I [7] _____ (run) from the kitchen to my bedroom.

**What [8] _____ you _____ (do) in your free time?**
I adore gardening.

**What are you doing now?**
I [9] _____ (shoot) a film set in Ireland. It's a political thriller.

**What's the best book you [10] _____ ever _____ (read)?**
_Talking with Angels_, by Gitta Mallasz.

**What's the worst thing anyone [11] _____ ever _____ (say) to you?**
I don't want to remember.

**[12] _____ you _____ (prefer) cats or dogs?**
I love them both.

**When [13] _____ you last _____ (cry)?**
Today, while I [14] _____ (rehearse). It's my job to bring emotions to life.

**What is your greatest achievement?**
It's not for me to say, but the film _Three Colours Blue_ is one of the best films I [15] _____ ever _____ (make).

**What is your motto on life?**
Don't look back. Live in the present. Here and now.

# Vocabulary

## 10 Phrasal verbs

**1** Complete the sentences with the verbs in the box.

| give | ~~find~~ | set | tidy | pick | take | slow |
|------|------|------|------|------|------|------|

1 Could you do me a favour? Could you **find** out the times of trains from London to Cambridge?

2 There was a terrible mess after the party. It took me ages to _____ everything up.

3 I have to be at the airport at 10.00, so I need to _____ off at about 8.00.

4 'What time does your plane _____ off?' 'Midday. Why?'

5 I'll give you a lift to the airport if you like. Why don't I _____ you up at about 9.30?

6 You can borrow my camera, but you must _____ it back to me.

7 You're driving too fast! _____ down!

**2** Complete the sentences with the particles in the box.

| up (x2) | back | off | away | out (x2) | ~~forward~~ |
|------|------|------|------|------|------|

1 I've heard so much about you. I'm really looking **forward** to meeting you.

2 Come _____! Don't walk away! I'm sorry if I upset you!

3 Hurry _____! If we don't go now, we'll miss the train!

4 I'll do your washing, but I refuse to put all your clothes _____ in your cupboards and drawers. You can do that yourself!

5 When I was five I fell _____ my horse and broke my arm.

6 My mother is always having arguments with people. She's fallen _____ with all her friends and most of the neighbours.

7 Sh! Don't make a noise or you'll wake the baby _____!

8 There are so many cheap restaurants in our town that we eat _____ most evenings.

# Reading

## 11 The greatest rock 'n' roll band in the world

**1** 🎧 Read the text quickly. Tick (✓) the song titles that you see.

1 ✓ Satisfaction
2 ☐ Get Off Of My Cloud
3 ☐ Not Fade Away
4 ☐ 19th Nervous Breakdown
5 ☐ Ruby Tuesday
6 ☐ Jumpin' Jack Flash
7 ☐ Honky Tonk Woman
8 ☐ Brown Sugar

**2** Read the text again. Are these sentences true (✓) or false (✗)? Correct the false sentences.

1 ✗ The band have been playing for nearly 50 years.
**The band have been playing for over 50 years.**

2 ☐ Two of them have known each other since school days.

3 ☐ They wanted a 'bad-boy' gang image to be like The Beatles.

4 ☐ They started touring when The Beatles stopped.

5 ☐ Ronnie Wood joined the band just before Brian Jones died.

6 ☐ Mick Jagger has never learnt to read music.

7 ☐ Both Mick Jagger and Keith Richards have been knighted.

8 ☐ They've never been to Russia.

**3** Who are the people in *italics* in these sentences?

1 *They* started the band.
   Mick Jagger, Keith Richards, and Brian Jones.

2 *He* plays the drums.
   _____

3 *They* stopped touring in 1966.
   _____

4 *He* drowned in a swimming pool.
   _____

5 *He* has seven children.
   _____

6 *He* appeared in a film.
   _____

7 *She* gave *him* a knighthood.
   _____

8 *They* watched The Stones at the Tsar's Winter Palace.
   _____

# The Rolling Stones

*– the greatest rock 'n' roll band in the world!*

**The Rolling Stones have been playing together for over 50 years, and for many people they are the 'Greatest Rock 'n' Roll Band in the world'.**

The group was formed in England in 1962 by school friends Mick Jagger and Keith Richards, along with guitarist Brian Jones. Later they were joined by Charlie Watts on drums and Bill Wyman on bass. They wanted a 'bad-boy' gang image in contrast to the most famous band of the time, The Beatles. They were soon pop idols with teenage fans all over Europe and America.

In 1964, they reached the UK Top 10 and the US Top 50 with 'Not Fade Away'. The 'bad boys' were on their way. 'Satisfaction' and '19th Nervous Breakdown', written by Jagger and Richards in 1965, are considered to be two of the greatest rock songs ever.

In 1966, The Beatles stopped touring, and The Stones started. They've been touring the world ever since and have continued to write great hits such as 'Jumpin' Jack Flash' (1968) and 'Honky Tonk Woman' (1969). However, with their fame came tragedy, caused by alcohol and drugs. Brian Jones became an addict and could no longer tour. In July 1969, he drowned in his own swimming pool. It was a painful time for The Stones, but they were still writing good songs. Their albums *Beggars Banquet* (1968) and *Sticky Fingers* (1971) were a huge success. Ronnie Wood joined the band in 1974, and during the 1970s they remained the biggest band in the world.

If Mick Jagger is the 'heart' of The Stones, then Keith Richards is 'the soul'. The two have survived ups and downs in their careers and personal lives. Mick can't even read music, but he has worked hard with Richards as songwriter, following the example of The Beatles' John Lennon and Paul McCartney.

Besides his music career, Mick has fathered seven children with four women and donated to numerous charities. He is now 'Sir Mick'! He was knighted by Queen Elizabeth II in 2003. Keith Richards has worked as an actor, appearing in the blockbuster movie *Pirates of the Caribbean* as the father of Jack Sparrow.

The Stones have made 55 albums and sold over 200 million records worldwide. They have played in all kinds of places from small clubs to huge stadiums. In 2007, they played in front of the Tsar's Winter Palace in St. Petersburg, Russia, for 50,000 fans. They have given more shows internationally than any other band in the world. Their last tour earned over $559 million.

Since the 1960s, The Rolling Stones have been touring the world, giving their audiences the kind of music they love – rock 'n' roll. And despite their age, The Rolling Stones is a better band now than it ever was.

***Long live rock 'n' roll – long live The Rolling Stones!***

## Listening

### 12 My kind of music

1  🎧 Listen to Amy and her mum. Answer the questions.

1  What is Amy's mum's favourite pop group?

_____

2  What kind of music does Amy's dad like?

_____

3  What kind of music does Amy like? What doesn't she like?

_____

4  What day of the week is it?

_____

2  Listen again. (Circle) the correct answer.

1  Amy Winehouse and Brian Jones were both *26 / 27* when they died.

2  The Rolling Stones are a *bit / lot* older than Amy's mum.

3  Amy *can / can't* imagine the world in 50 years time.

4  Amy is *15 / 16* years old.

5  Amy's dad *was / wasn't* a big fan of The Beatles.

6  Amy *makes fun of / really likes* her dad's music.

7  When Amy was little she *laughed / screamed* if her parents played their favourite music.

# Pronunciation

## 13 Words that sound the same

Some words sound the same, but they are spelt differently and have different meanings. They are called homophones.

/miːt/ *meet*  Let's meet at six.
/miːt/ *meat*  Do you eat meat?

**1** 🎧 Listen and tick (✓) the word that sounds the same as the word on the left.

| 1 | fair | /feə(r)/ | ☐ fear | ☐ fire | ✓ fare |
|---|------|----------|--------|--------|--------|
| 2 | been | /biːn/ | ☐ bean | ☐ bin | ☐ Ben |
| 3 | know | /nəʊ/ | ☐ now | ☐ no | ☐ new |
| 4 | where | /weə(r)/ | ☐ war | ☐ were | ☐ wear |
| 5 | hear | /hɪə(r)/ | ☐ here | ☐ her | ☐ hair |
| 6 | wait | /weɪt/ | ☐ what | ☐ wet | ☐ weight |
| 7 | caught | /kɔːt/ | ☐ cut | ☐ court | ☐ coat |
| 8 | piece | /piːs/ | ☐ peace | ☐ peas | ☐ pies |

**2** 🎧 Listen and write the other spelling of the word in phonetic script.

1 /wʊd/ *would* and _____
2 /bluː/ *blew* and _____
3 /wiːk/ *weak* and _____
4 /θruː/ *through* and _____
5 /rəʊd/ *rode* and _____
6 /nəʊz/ *knows* and _____
7 /baɪ/ *by* and _____
8 /sɔː(r)/ *sore* and _____

**3** 🎧 Listen and complete the sentences with the correct spelling of the phonetic script in brackets.

1 I'm not very well. I've got a _____ (/sɔː(r)/) throat.
  I've _____ (/biːn/) off work for a _____ (/wiːk/).

2 I want to lose _____ (/weɪt/), so I won't have another _____ (/piːs/) of cake, thank you.

3 That's a lovely _____ (/bluː/) dress. _____ (/weə(r)/) did you _____ (/baɪ/) it?

4 The boys _____ (/rəʊd/) their bikes along the _____ (/rəʊd/) to school.

5 We walked _____ (/θruː/) the dark _____ (/wʊd/) then out into the lovely sun.

6 He _____ (/θruː/) the ball high into the air and I _____ (/kɔːt/) it.

# *Just for fun!*

## 14 Crossword – people in the arts

Complete the crossword. The answers are all people in the arts and entertainment industry.

Across (grid with answer: ¹C O ²M E D I A N)

**Across**
1 Someone who tells jokes to make us laugh. (8)
3 Mick Jagger is a _____. (6)
6 Nureyev was a ballet _____. (6)
8 Juliette Binoche is an _____. (7)
9 Johnny Depp is an _____. (5)
11 Charlie Watts is a _____. (7)
12 Someone who writes novels. (8)
13 Shakespeare was a _____. (10)

**Down**
2 Pianists and violinists are _____. (9)
4 Keith Richards is a _____. (9)
5 Picasso was an _____. (7)
7 Beethoven was a _____. (8)
10 Someone who writes poems. (4)

# 12

First conditional • *might* • Second conditional
• Prepositions • Pronunciation – word stress

**Just wondering …**

# First conditional

## 1 Choosing the correct form

Look at the holiday brochure. Complete the text with the phrases in the box.

| 'll enjoy | 'll put | ~~like swimming~~ | 'll want to go | enjoy | book | 'll give |

## Sun Tours — Holidays to remember

### Something for everyone!

- If your kids ¹ **like swimming** and playing on the beach, they'll love the long, sandy beaches.
- If you ² _____ fine food and wine, you'll want to dine at our award-winning restaurants.
- If you need to relax and want to treat yourself, you ³ _____ spending time at our fabulous spa facilities.
- If you want history and culture, you ⁴ _____ on one of the many excursions we offer.

### Our promises to you!

- If you ⁵ _____ before the end of the month, we'll give you a discount of 5%.
- We ⁶ _____ a free bottle of champagne in your room when you arrive.
- If you aren't satisfied with your holiday, we ⁷ _____ you your money back!

*Get the best holiday at the best price!*

## 2 Questions and answers

1 Your friend is going on holiday. Write questions about possible problems.

1 What/do/you/miss/plane? **What will you do if you miss the plane?**

2 What/do/plane/be/delayed? _____

3 What/do/hotels/be/full? _____

4 What/do/you/not like/food? _____

5 What/do/you/get/sunburnt? _____

6 Where/go/beaches/be/crowded? _____

2 Match the answers with a question in exercise 1.

a ☐ I'll just eat bread and fruit.

b ☐ I won't sunbathe for a few days.

c ☑ I won't miss it. I'll get there in time.

d ☐ I'll find a youth hostel.

e ☐ I'll just have to wait at the airport.

f ☐ I'll go to the hotel swimming pool.

## 3 Conjunctions

**1** Complete the sentences with *if* or *when*.

1 _____ you can't do your homework, ask for help.

2 I'll pay you back _____ I next see you.

3 I'm going to bed _____ the film ends.

4 Come on! _____ we don't hurry, we'll miss the bus!

5 _____ anyone phones me, tell them I'm out.

6 I always get excited _____ summer comes.

7 _____ the weather's bad, we'll stay at home.

**2** Andy is saying goodbye to his wife, Beth, who is going away on a business trip. Put the verbs in brackets into the correct tense and (circle) the correct words in *italics*.

**A** Bye, darling! Have a good trip!

**B** Thanks. I **'ll call** (call) you (*when*) / *while* I arrive at the hotel.

**A** But I'm going out tonight. Remember?

**B** Well, *when* / *if* you _____ (be) out when I _____ (call), I _____ (leave) a message on the answer phone.

**A** Great. What time do you think you'll be there?

**B** *If* / *When* the plane _____ (arrive) on time, I _____ (be) at the hotel at about 10.00 in the evening your time.

**A** OK. I hope everything goes well. Let me know *when* / *while* you _____ (have) the time of your flight home, and I _____ (pick) you up at the airport.

**B** Right! Have a nice time *as soon as* / *while* I _____ (be) away! Don't miss me too much!

## *might*

### 4 *might = perhaps + will*

Rewrite the sentences using *might*.

1 Perhaps it'll rain tomorrow.
   **It might rain tomorrow.**

2 Perhaps we'll go to Spain on holiday.
   _____

3 Perhaps I'll go out tonight.
   _____

4 Perhaps Jane will invite me to her party.
   _____

5 Perhaps I'll get some money for my birthday.
   _____

## 5 Choosing the correct form

(Circle) the correct form of the verb in *italics*.

1 Don't wait for me. I'*ll be* / *might* be late. It depends on the traffic.

2 'What are you doing tonight?'
   'I don't know. I'*m going out* / *might go out*, or I *might stay in* / *'m staying in*.'

3 'Bye! I'*ll see* / *might see* you this evening!'
   'See you later! Dinner will be ready at 7.00.'

4 'What are you cooking tonight?'
   'I haven't decided yet. I'*m going to make* / *might make* a lasagne.'

5 I *might take* / *'m taking* Joe to the theatre for his birthday. I booked it last night.

6 Beccy and Stefan *are going to get married* / *might get married*! They got engaged last week.

# Second conditional

## 6 Dreams

**Jamie's real life**

- He lives at home with his parents.
- He gets up at 6.00 a.m.
- He drives an old second-hand car.
- He works ten hours a day.
- He never has a holiday.
- He usually wears scruffy jeans and a T-shirt.

**1** Jamie works in a factory. Read about his real life, then complete the sentences about his dreams.

1 'I _**'d live**_ in a lovely big house!'

2 'I _____ at midday!'

3 'I _____ a Porsche!'

4 'I _____ long hours – just four hours a day!'

5 'I _____ on holiday to Hawaii!'

6 'I _____ a designer suit!'

**2** Write the questions about Jamie's dreams.

1 ' _**Where would he live?**_ '   'In a big house.'

2 '_____?'   'At midday.'

3 '_____?'   'A Porsche.'

4 '_____?'   'Four hours a day.'

5 '_____?'   'To Hawaii.'

6 '_____?'   'A designer suit.'

## 7 If things were different …

Look at the facts about Laura. Then complete the sentences below, using the second conditional.

1 **Fact:** Laura lives in the centre of town.

If she _**lived**_ (live) in the country, she _**'d have**_ (have) a dog.

2 **Fact:** She doesn't have a dog.

If she _____ (have) a dog, she _____ (go) for walks.

3 **Fact:** She doesn't have a garden.

If she _____ (have) a garden, she _____ (grow) vegetables.

4 **Fact:** She never has any free time.

If she _____ (have) free time, she _____ (take up) painting.

## 8 First or second conditional?

**1** (Circle) the correct form of the verb in *italics*.

1 If I *am / were* younger, I'*ll travel / 'd travel* the world.

2 When I *see / saw* Jack, I'*ll tell / 'd tell* him I spoke to you.

3 Are you going out? I'*ll come / 'd come* with you if you *liked / like*.

4 If you *came / come* from my country, you'*ll understand / 'd understand* the problem.

5 If my children *are / were* as naughty as hers, I'*ll be / 'd be* ashamed.

**2** Put the verbs in brackets into the correct form.

1 What _____ you _____ (do) if you _____ (win) a lot of money?

2 If I _____ (be) taller, I _____ (join) the police force.

3 We _____ (go) swimming if the weather _____ (be) nice.

4 I _____ (buy) the jeans if they _____ (be) cheaper, but £80 is too much!

5 If my English _____ (be) better next year, I _____ (go) on holiday to the US.

6 If I _____ (speak) perfect English, I _____ (not have to) study at all!

## Reading

### 9 Sleep – where would we be without it?

**1** 🎧 Read the text quickly. Answer the questions.

1 What *don't* scientists know? What *do* they know?

_____

2 How much of our lives do we sleep?

_____

3 If you suffer from *Fatal Familial Insomnia*, what can't you do?

_____

4 What did Napoleon and Alexander the Great have in common?

_____

5 Why did a Frenchman kill his wife?

_____

# Sleep
## *where would we be without it?*

**Believe it or not, there is a 'World Sleep Day'. This year its slogan was '*Sleep Well, Grow Healthy*'.**

Scientists don't know exactly why we need sleep. But one thing they do know is that if we didn't sleep, we'd die. It's as though we need a period of time each day when we don't have to process lots of new information. Our brain can go into shutdown mode, and we can experience a different sort of reality.

Most people sleep for about a third of their lives. That is about seven hours a day. Of this, 55–60% is light sleep, then 15–25% is deeper sleep, and 20–25% is Rapid Eye Movement (REM) sleep. In REM, your body relaxes completely, but your brain is awake. Dreams occur in all stages of sleep, but REM dreams are the most lively and colourful. They are the ones we try to hold on to when we first wake up, but the harder we try the quicker they disappear.

However, there are some people who never sleep. They suffer from a rare illness called *Fatal Familial Insomnia*. Michael Corke, a music teacher from Chicago, suffered from this. He died

in 1993 at the age of 42, having not slept for six months. He didn't even sleep when doctors tried to put him into a coma.

Sleeplessness has always been fatal. The Romans killed Macedonian King Perseus in 168 BC, simply by keeping him awake.

### *'We don't need sleep!'*

Some people boast about how little sleep they need. Thomas Edison slept for three to four hours a night. He said: 'A man doesn't need any sleep.'

British Prime Minister, Margaret Thatcher, said it was a weakness to need more than four hours' sleep.

**2** Read the text again. (Circle) the correct answer.

1 There are *three / four* stages of sleep.

2 In REM sleep your *brain / body* relaxes, but your *brain / body* doesn't relax.

3 Michael Corke finally died *from lack of sleep / after being put into a coma*.

4 Thomas Edison and Margaret Thatcher never slept for more than *three / four* hours a night.

5 Peter Trip was a *music teacher / disc jockey*. He stayed awake for over *eight / ten* days.

6 *Epimenides the Wise / Sancho Panza* said, 'God bless the inventor of sleep.'

**3** What do these numbers refer to?

| | | | |
|---|---|---|---|
| 1 7 _____ | 3 1993 _____ | 5 201 _____ |
| 2 15–25 _____ | 4 168 _____ | 6 57 _____ |

Napoleon took short naps on his horse. Similarly, Alexander the Great didn't sleep much at night but prepared for battle by taking daytime naps. The American DJ Peter Tripp set a record in 1959 when he stayed awake for 201 hours in a glass studio in Times Square, New York.

However, most people believe that a good night's sleep makes you feel better. It is said that in 600BC, Epimenides the Wise, one of the 'Seven Wise Men of Greece', slept for 57 years. When he woke up, he was wise. And, there is the story of a Frenchman, who, when asked why he had murdered his wife, replied truthfully, 'She woke me up, so I killed her.'

We know that if we didn't sleep at all we would die, but do we *need* to sleep so much? Or do we just *like* to sleep? Who really knows?

> *'While I sleep I have no fear, nor hope, nor trouble, nor glory. God bless the inventor of sleep.'*
> **Sancho Panza, *Don Quixote*, by Miguel de Cervantes**

## Listening

### 10 The meaning of dreams

**1** 🎧 Listen to four people talking about their dreams. Write what they dream about. Choose from the words in the box. You don't need to use them all.

> flying   a horse   a bird   a house   family
> school   love

Robert    Sonia

1 _____    2 _____

Harry    Lucy

3 _____    4 _____

**2** 🎧 Listen again. Complete the sentences about the dreams.

Robert

1 The _____ were chasing Robert down the _____ .

2 His wife said, 'You've never had a _____ . Go back to _____ !'

Sonia

3 Sonia saw a _____ she'd never seen before.

4 The light in the _____ wasn't _____ .

Harry

5 Harry realized that he hadn't done any _____ for his exam.

6 When he woke up his _____ was pounding.

Lucy

7 She can push down on her _____ and go up in the _____ .

8 It's a wonderful _____ when she looks down on the _____ below.

# Vocabulary

## 11 Prepositions

Complete the sentences with the correct preposition.

### Verb + preposition

1 Look **at** the sunset! Isn't it fantastic!

2 I'm looking _____ Mary. Have you seen her?

3 Can I talk _____ you for a moment?

4 I agree _____ you about most things but not politics.

5 I'll pay _____ the coffees. You bought lunch.

6 I'm thinking _____ living in France for a year.

### Preposition + noun

1 What's **on** TV tonight?

2 My flat is _____ the fifth floor.

3 I opened your letter _____ accident.

4 I'm a bit busy _____ the moment. Can you call back?

5 _____ my opinion, all politicians are liars.

6 I always get to work _____ time. I'm never late.

### Adjective + preposition

1 Are you interested _____ modern art?

2 I'm very angry _____ you. Why didn't you phone me?

3 I've been so worried _____ you.

4 The town is full _____ tourists in the summer.

5 I'm so proud _____ my children. I think they're great!

6 We're so excited _____ our holiday! We're going to Greece.

### Noun + preposition

1 I've got a present _____ you. Happy birthday!

2 Can I have a word _____ you for a minute?

3 Would you like to see a photo _____ my children?

4 We've got an invitation _____ your ex-girlfriend's wedding! Hm!

5 The advantage _____ living in a town is that everything is nearby.

6 Congratulations _____ your exam results! You must feel delighted!

# Pronunciation

## 12 Word stress

🎧 Listen to the word stress of the words in the box. Write the words in the correct box.

| | | | |
|---|---|---|---|
| ~~lottery~~ | understand | wallet | envelope |
| president | advantage | decision | universe |
| agree | ambitious | direction | forever |
| system | ocean | accident | business |
| remember | practice | musician | programme |
| award | passionate | different | reply |
| happiness | divorced | entertain | become |

● ● ●

lottery

● ● ●

● ● ●

● ●

● ●

# Just for fun!

## 13 Crossword – about me

Complete the crossword. The clues are in the text about a student of English.

I've _____ (18 across) learning English for several years now, and I think my English is _____ (11 down) better. I've _____ (5 down) a lot of new words, and I don't _____ (14 down) as many mistakes. I always do my homework very _____ (12 across), and my teacher says I'm a very good student!

I enjoy _____ (1 down) English very much. It's an _____ (16 across) language – people from all over the world speak English when they're together. In a lot of jobs it's _____ (17 across) to speak English well. I want to work in tourism.

I've been to England once. Two years _____ (15 down) I went to London for a holiday. I _____ (2 across) with a family in Chelsea. They were called Mr and Mrs Brown, and they _____ (9 across) after me really well. They showed me all the tourist sights. We went on the London Eye, and I saw Big Ben, the Houses of Parliament, and Buckingham _____ (6 down). I thought the people were very _____ (4 across) – very kind and helpful. My English improved a lot _____ (8 across) I was in London.

Next year I'm _____ (13 down) to continue with my English classes. I'm looking _____ (7 across) to being an intermediate student! There are lots of things I can do _____ (10 down) – there are some great websites with interviews, videos, and exercises.

But before that it's the summer holidays! I'm going to read books, swim, and _____ (3 down) on the beach – I love the sun! I can't wait.

18 across: B E E N

# Tapescripts

## UNIT 1

**Exercise 11, parts 1 and 2**

### Andy and Ed

**A = Andy   E = Ed**

**A** Hey Ed, aren't you getting married soon?

**E** Yeah, next month.

**A** Are you nervous?

**E** Yes, definitely. It's a big step. You're a happily married man. What's your secret for a happy marriage?

**A** No big secret. It's love. We just fell in love.

**E** So … , was it love at first sight?

**A** Nearly. I was just 21 and at this boring party. I wanted to leave then I saw this girl – Janice – come into the room with a friend.

**E** Another girl?

**A** No, a boy. He was a friend but not a boyfriend, if you know what I mean. At least that's what she told me. I could see she was bored with him. Anyway, our eyes met, and she just walked over. We chatted all evening till the party finished at midnight, and it all started from there really.

**E** What happened to the 'boyfriend'?

**A** I have no idea. I never saw him again. The best thing was that when we talked we discovered that we had, and still have, so many things in common.

**E** Like what?

**A** Well, music of course. She's a great singer, and I play the guitar.

**E** Oh, of course, you two do gigs together.

**A** Well, now we have the kids we don't do as many gigs as before.

**E** Oh, yes, you have twins, don't you? Wow!

**A** Yeah … It was really difficult when we first had the twins. Janice couldn't travel abroad with me on work trips any more. I felt bad about going away, but she was really good about it.

**E** Huh! Marriage! There's lots to think about.

**A** Are you having a big wedding?

**E** Huge! 200 people!

**A** Good luck, Ed. I'm sure it'll be a fantastic day. Just try to enjoy it. I enjoyed my wedding a lot. It was small but really romantic.

## UNIT 2

**Exercise 10, parts 1 and 2**

### The best things in life are free

**K = Kirstie   F = Fiona   N = Nigel   B = Ben**

**K** Mum, muum, can I have a new …?

**F** No, you can't. Nothing else today. You're always asking for things.

**N** Sssh Kirstie, you can't have everything you want when you want it. We can't afford it. Come on now, let's think of some of the things we have in our family that are free. What's the best thing for you, Ben?

**B** Er – What's the best free thing? I know, it's my dog.

**K** It's my dog too …

**B** OK, it's our dog, Boris. He's the nicest member of our family. He cost nothing because he came from the dogs' home. He's the best thing because, em … I love taking him for walks. I love the crazy way he runs around the park and the fields.

**K** I love him too. I love the way he just loves us. Do you all want to know what my best free thing is?

**B** Huh! I'm sure you'll tell us.

**K** Well, it's Amy.

**N and F** Aaah! How nice. We all love Amy.

**K** But I think she loves me best! And I love her because she always laughs when she sees me, and she holds out her hands for me to pick her up. And her first word was my name, she says 'K, K, K' .

**B** That's the only word she says. She says it for everything and everyone.

**K** No, she doesn't. She …

**B** SSh Kirst! What about you dad? What's your best free thing?

**N** That's easy. All day long I work in the dirty, noisy city, among crowds of people … so my best thing is when we all go walking in the countryside at the weekend.

**K** I hate walking!

**N** I know you do … but it's good to do things for others. The reason I love it is … well, it makes me so happy when we go for walks as a family and take Boris and a picnic. I love eating outdoors. Food tastes better.

**K** Oh, yeah, I love the picnics. What about you mum?

**F** Ooh, there are lots of things I like that don't cost anything. There's my family of course – er no, perhaps not, they cost a lot – 'specially you Kirstie.

**K** That's not fair. I don't …

**B** Sssh! Go on mum.

**F** Let's see … what do I like? I know – er, the first signs of spring because I love to see the trees turning green and the garden coming to life after winter. I find it exciting every year. Oh … and sunsets. That's another thing I love. There's nothing more beautiful than a glorious red sunset at the end of the day.

**K** Boring!

**N** Don't be rude Kirstie! I think your mother and I like the same kind of things. One day you'll change your mind. The best things aren't always the things you buy.

## UNIT 3

**Exercise 9**

### Someone stole my bag!

**P = Policeman   M = Margot Clements**

**P** Good morning, Madam. Can I help you?

**M** Oh, yes. Hello officer. Oh dear, it's terrible. I'm still shaking.

**P** Now try and calm down and tell me what happened.

**M** OK. I'll try. Well I was walking along the High Street and – er I was hot so I took off my jacket and er … I was carrying it in my right hand, I think, no, it was my left hand, yes, my left, and then suddenly my mobile phone rang. I heard it ring, but I couldn't find it in my bag and …

**P** Now, please slow down and first tell me your name and address?

**M** Oh, sorry. It's Mrs Clements, Margot Clements, and I live at 13 Marlins Close, Potten End.

**P** Thank you Mrs Clements. Now, you were carrying your jacket, and you were looking for your phone in your bag, yes?

**M** Yes. Oh, and it's a new phone. I only got it two days ago.

**P** Could you please tell me what happened?

**M** Of course, sorry. Mmmm … I couldn't find my phone so I stopped walking and put my bag on a bench to have a proper look. I wasn't holding my bag, 'cos my jacket was in the other hand, and my mobile, it was … it was still ringing, – er … and then suddenly there was this man, he was walking towards me and as he passed he picked up my bag and ran off. Oh, it was awful … He took my bag, my mobile … it was still ringing … he took everything. It all happened so quickly.

**P** I know, these things are very upsetting. Did you see the man? What did he look like?

**M** Well, unfortunately I didn't get a good look. It was all so quick, but I think he was quite

young – about 18 or 20, and he had long
brown hair.

**M** Did you see what he was wearing?

**M** Mmmmmm. I think he was wearing blue jeans and a t-shirt – a red T-shirt, I think.

**P** And … what time did the incident occur?

**M** Oh! It happened 20 minutes ago at 1 o'clock.

**P** Could you describe your bag please and tell me what's in it?

**M** It's quite big – er – not very big. It's grey and black with lots of pockets – that's why I couldn't find my phone – too many pockets! My purse was in the bag – it's blue – and there was £50 in it … er … and my driving licence. Oh dear! And my house keys! They were in the bag too!

**P** Well, Margot, it's your lucky day! Someone handed in a handbag fitting that description just 10 minutes ago. The thief obviously dropped it as he was running away. But please be more careful in future. Keep a tight hold of your bag.

**M** Oh thank you officer. That's fantastic! What a relief.

# UNIT 4

## Exercise 11

### My favourite kind of meal

**Dave**

My favourite food is my mum's home cooking. I like everything she makes, but the thing I miss most when I'm away from home is mum's roast dinner on a Sunday. It's my favourite because my mum's Sunday dinners are the best in the world. She always cooks a roast – lamb, pork, chicken – but my favourite is roast beef with roast potatoes and Yorkshire pudding, and usually a green vegetable – broccoli, I don't like that so much, or peas – I like peas – and then some of her delicious gravy poured over it all. Fabulous!

**Sally**

My favourite food is egg and tomato sandwiches … BUT … I only really eat them when I go for picnics in the summer. I like them so much because I love eating food outdoors – when you're in the countryside, sitting in a field or by a river, it tastes fantastic whatever it is. But egg and tomato sandwiches taste best of all. They're simple and delicious. Just chopped eggs and tomatoes mixed with a bit of mayonnaise and some salt and pepper in white sliced bread. Yummy! It's no good eating them in the house or in the garden. They only taste good in the open air in the summer sunshine.

**Freddie**

I know it's terrible … but … my favourite meal is hamburgers and chips. And I only like the hamburgers from places like McDonalds and Burger King. I think it's because I ate so many when I was a kid. I loved them then, and I still do! I really love the Big Mac with all the trimmings – a big juicy burger, cheese, gherkins and some salad, not a lot, and a big portion of chips with ketchup. I go to a Maccy D's two or three times a week. I don't tell my girlfriend – she thinks I'm mad!

**Lizzie**

I learnt to cook my favourite meal when I was living in East Africa – a delicious chicken curry! I had friends from all over the world there, but I worked with two Asian sisters, and their mum was a fantastic cook. When I tasted her curry I couldn't believe how good it was, so the girls asked their mum to show me how to make it. You mix lots of spices with garlic, a little tomato paste, and yoghurt – the chicken cooks in this with fried onions and potatoes on top. You eat it with boiled rice. I still make it when I have friends for supper. It's my favourite because it doesn't taste like the curries in Indian restaurants. It's quite different. Everyone loves it.

# UNIT 5

## Exercise 14, parts 1 and 2

### Three teenagers and their ambitions

**Frankie Meazza, 17**

I lived with my mum until she married again. I didn't get on with my stepdad, we fought all the time, so I left. At first I slept in friends' houses, but then I got a place in this hostel. It's really OK here, not too bad at all. I have lots of new friends, and I'm now studying for my exams. I really want to make something of my life. I'd really like to be a mechanic and work with cars. Cars are my passion. I'm learning to drive at the moment. I'm thinking of joining the army. That's because you get good training in the army, but it's not easy to get in. I'm going to try though.

**Isabel Blair, 18**

A few years ago, when I was about 14 or 15, my mum and dad were really worried about me. I was so lazy. I just wanted to be with my friends all the time, and I didn't do my schoolwork. But mum and dad were cool, they didn't get angry. Dad just said 'You're a bright girl but a silly girl. You're throwing away your chances.' And, finally, I thought OK, he's right. So I started to work hard, and now I've got good exam results. I don't know what I want to study yet, so I'm going to give myself a year to think about it. I have cousins in Canada, so I'm going to stay with them for a few months. I'd like to get a job over there if I can. My uncle owns and runs two care homes in Toronto for retired people. I hope to work there. I'm really looking forward to going.

**James Owen, 17**

I know exactly what I want to do. You see, my dad died four years ago, when I was 13. He was ill for a couple of years – it was a really difficult time. But the doctors and nurses were so wonderful looking after him that I decided that I wanted to be a doctor. I'm studying for my final school exams at the moment. I hope to do well. My teachers say that they think I will. If I get good grades, I'm going to Newcastle University to study medicine. It's a long and difficult course and a lot of my friends can't imagine studying for six more years, but I really want to do it. I know I can. I'd like to be a surgeon eventually. I want to make my mum proud – she says she's proud already. She says,

'Go for it, James. You'll be a great doctor.' She's lovely, my mum.

# UNIT 6

## Exercise 9, parts 1 and 2

### Visiting London

**A** We're from Australia. It's our first time in London. We arrived a week ago, and I think we know London pretty well already.

**B** Nah, not really – we know the tourists' spots. London's a huge city – we only know the centre.

**A** Well, we thought a bus tour was the best way to start, so we took a tour of all the best-known landmarks. It was called 'The Big Bus Tour'. It was open top, and we sat upstairs and …

**B** It didn't rain thank goodness, but it was cold on top of that bus.

**A** Yeah, but we saw so much – it was amazing. We saw all these places that you know about from pictures and on TV and in the movies. We began at Piccadilly Circus and …

**B** Yeah, the Statue of Eros was a lot smaller than I thought.

**A** Yeah it was, but I thought it was cute. There were lots of people sitting round it on the steps. You know they say if you stand in Piccadilly Circus long enough, you'll meet nearly everyone you ever knew.

**B** I don't believe that …

**A** Well, that's what they say. Next stop was Trafalgar Square – Nelson's Column was as big as I expected.

**B** Yeah, it was. Lots of people sitting round there too.

**A** And I loved the drive down the Mall to Buckingham Palace. But the flag wasn't up, so we knew the Queen wasn't there.

**B** She was probably in one of her other palaces. I think she has a few.

**A** I liked Big Ben and the Houses of Parliament. Big Ben was big, and it was striking eleven when we drove past. What did you think of Big Ben?

**B** Yeah, good. But I liked the London Eye more. It's right by the river there. We're going on it tomorrow.

**A** You get the best views in London from the Eye.

**B** I read that, and I also read that 4 million people a year go on it. It's the most popular tourist attraction.

**A** Really? More popular than the museums and galleries?

**B** Yup.

**A** But do you know what I liked best?

**B** Seeing Westminster Abbey where Prince William and Kate married?

**A** That was interesting, but best for me are the parks. We have a Hyde Park in Sydney, Australia, and I love the one in London too. There are parks everywhere, so when you just can't walk another step seeing the sights, you can sit down on a bench or some grass in the park.

**B** Well, you can if it's not raining. Yeah, I liked the parks too.

# UNIT 7

**Exercise 11, parts 1–3**

## Till death us do part

### Ethel and Norman

**I = Interviewer   E = Ethel   N = Norman**

**I** Congratulations on your golden wedding anniversary!

**E** Thank you so much …

**N** Well, thank you. It makes us feel very proud to say we've been married for 50 years.

**E** Time goes so fast. When you're first married, a year seems a long time. But then you have kids, the kids grow up, and suddenly they've left home …

**I** Was that difficult? When it was just the two of you …?

**E** Oh, no. We've always been best friends, so we have lots of things to do together.

**I** Do you ever argue about anything? You know, have a few bad words …?

**N** Sure, we have arguments! But then we say sorry.

**I** Tell me … where did you two meet?

**N** We met at a dance on a Saturday night …

**E** I saw this good-looking boy on the other side of the room …

**N** Oh, I saw her as soon as she walked in. It took me a while to ask her to dance.

**E** We started going out together, and two years later we got married.

**I** And … where did you live?

**E** We bought a house – a lovely semi-detached with a nice garden – and we've lived in the same area all our married life.

**I** Wow! So you've never moved away?

**N** No, we've always lived around here.

**E** He's the only boyfriend I've ever had, and he's the only man I've ever loved.

**N** Daft old thing!

### Shirley Meldon

**I = Interviewer   S = Shirley**

**I** I'm sorry that you and Bruce didn't make your golden wedding anniversary …

**S** That's all right. It's been a couple of years now … Bruce died two years ago, so I've … I've been on my own now for two years. It was very difficult at first.

**I** How long … were you married?

**S** We were married for 48 years, so that's not bad, is it?

**I** It's very good!

**S** We were childhood sweethearts. We met at school when we were both 16, and he was the only man I ever loved.

**I** 48 years … is an awfully long time. What do you think is the secret of a good marriage?

**S** It's easy. You keep trying. Don't give in! Every marriage has its ups and downs.

**I** Did you argue? Did you and Bruce ever have arguments …?

**S** No, we didn't. We never had an argument about anything. Not once.

**I** That's incredible! How have you found living without Bruce? You said it was hard …

**S** It was awful. I can't tell you how hard it was. But time goes by, and each day, each month gets a little easier.

**I** And you've moved house!

**S** Yes. We lived in a cottage near the sea, and it was beautiful. But it was too big for just me. So I've moved to a flat in a small town. It's much more convenient. It isn't as pretty, but it's better for someone my age.

**I** Well, you look fantastic to me!

**S** Thank you! That's so kind!

# UNIT 8

**Exercise 11**

## The train driver

**I = Interviewer   S = Sue**

**I** Sue, how long have you been a train driver?

**S** I've been a driver now for over four years.

**I** Do you earn a good salary?

**S** I earn about £37,000 a year. That's without Sundays. If I work Sundays, I get paid more!!

**I** What's the best thing about the job?

**S** It's obvious. I love trains, and it's amazing earning money for driving them. But … maybe the best part is the kids who wave from bridges or fields as we go past. They are so excited when they see the trains, especially if you sound your horn! I remember doing the same when I was small.

**I** Are there any disadvantages?

**S** The hours. I have to work a 35 hour week. But this is at different times. Sometimes I have to start work at two in the morning, but then I finish before lunch. Other days I have to start at eleven at night when the rest of the world is going to bed.

**I** How did you become a train driver?

**S** By accident. I was a shop manager at a clothes shop. I hated it. A friend's wife who worked for the railway said I should try that, so I did. I took a job as a ticket inspector! I loved it, and after six months a colleague told me that I should take the exam to be a driver – I passed, and I never looked back!

**I** Do you meet any interesting people?

**S** Sometimes you meet famous people. I've met TV stars, and lots of politicians use the railway.

**I** Do you have to wear a uniform?

**S** Yes, I do, and it's awful, really awful, but it has to be really … you can't look like an air hostess if you have to climb in and out of trains.

**I** Is it difficult for a woman in what is usually a man's job?

**S** It's OK. Of course most of the drivers are men, but we're all good friends. Sometimes they make fun of me, but I give as good as I get.

**I** What's your advice to young women who are interested in the job?

**S** There are now quite a few female drivers, but we need more. So, I'd say 'go for it' if you are interested, but don't think that it's going to be a glamorous job. It's exciting but not glamorous … you'll probably hate the uniform! But it's a great job and the money isn't bad either!

# UNIT 9

**Exercise 7**

## A love story

**P = Peter   A = Amanda**

**P** Hello, Amanda.

**A** Peter!

**P** I'm surprised you recognized me.

**A** Really? Have you moved back here?

**P** Good heavens no. I work in London now. I've come back for my dad's 70th birthday. He's having a huge party.

**A** That's great. I'm sure it'll be a lot of fun.

**P** And your parents? Are they well?

**A** Fine. They're excited about my sister's wedding tomorrow. That's why I'm back in town.

**P** That's nice. Are you in a hurry?

**A** No, not really.

**P** Well, let's go for a coffee.

**A** So, Peter. Did you travel the world?

**P** Ah no, I didn't. I studied law instead. I'm a lawyer.

**A** Do you enjoy it?

**P** Yes, I do. And what about you? Do you still paint? I loved your paintings.

**A** I haven't painted anything for years. I've just had a few temporary jobs in offices. Oh Peter, I don't know why I left you that day.

**P** It's OK. We were very young, too young. It happens. People break up.

**A** Yes, you're right. Well, I must go. I have to help mum with the flowers for the wedding. Goodbye Peter.

**P** Bye, Amanda. Nice to see you.

# UNIT 10

**Exercise 8, parts 1–3**

## Internet dating disasters

### Cathy's story: Too good to be true

This was last summer. I was bored, and I was at home with the parents before going back to music college, so I thought I'd like to try Internet dating.

I started emailing this guy called Tim, and he seemed just fine online. We had some pretty good conversations on the phone as well. After a few days we arranged a first date – a meal in an expensive French restaurant. It sounded good. I couldn't wait.

So date night came, and he arrived in this fabulous car. Now, here is the only good part, he was better looking than his photograph. He was really good-looking, film-star good looks. But … then he started driving – so fast. And he began shouting, 'Go, go, go!' and swearing. There was no conversation just loud rock music as we raced along. He'd told me, before we met, that he loved Vivaldi and the classics. LIAR!

The rest of the night was just more speeding, more awful loud music. There was no French restaurant. He took me to a drive-through, a hamburger place, and he had a huge hamburger. I didn't want anything. He said, 'Come on! It's the best. It's real 'cowboy food'.

I told him to take me home. And thank goodness he did. Never again. He lied about everything.

### Michelle's story: Nightmare meeting

I was chatting online to this guy for about 6 months. I felt that we were actually falling in love. We sent lots of photos of each other, and soon were talking and texting everyday. Finally, we decided to meet in a hotel bar. I didn't want to go alone, so I took my sister.

We walked into the bar, and I was shocked. The person smiling at me from the bar didn't look like the person in the photos. He was a guy in his early 50s. He was wearing a pair of shorts, tennis shoes, and a football shirt with a baseball cap turned backwards. I was horrified … and he had thick, round glasses. I couldn't believe it. Then he said. 'I've got something to show you. Look at these.' And he got out some pictures of his wife and family, 'Aren't my kids the cutest?' My sister and I looked at each other, said nothing, turned, and ran out of the bar. It was wonderful to be outside – we couldn't stop laughing all the way home. I'm so glad she came with me.

### Adrian's story: It wasn't in the stars

I posted an ad, really just for fun. One reply seemed interesting. I responded, and we chatted online for a while, and then on the phone. The normal 'getting to know you' stuff. Eventually, we arranged a date. Just a movie and maybe dinner. Well, she looked OK – quite pretty – and we had fun at the movie and decided to go for a meal and chat some more. It was here it started to go wrong. I found out that she also talks to my cousin online, and all she wanted to do was to talk about him. Not only was she talking about another guy, but one related to me! I was a bit annoyed. But, after the meal we talked some more and then walked to a nice park with a wonderful view of the river. She said, 'Isn't this romantic?' Then she asked me about my birthday. 'That's nice,' I thought … but she became really quiet and suddenly she said: 'I don't think we can see each other again.' I didn't understand. 'Why not?' 'Because I'm a Scorpio, and you're a Gemini. It won't work.' Well, I sometimes read my horoscope, but I don't use it to see who to date!

So that was it. The end. But note this, she did eventually date my cousin. He's a Virgo.

### Shona's story: Mr Ego

A guy called Michael responded to my ad. He sent a picture of a nice-looking man in his 20s. We chatted on the phone a bit. He said he was a 'world famous artist and author.' So, I tried to look him up on the Internet. I couldn't find any information about him. But I was a little bored, so I decided to meet him for dinner and drinks during the week. He picked a really expensive restaurant. He arrived late. He came towards me saying, 'Darling, I'm so sorry. I had a meeting with my publisher.' He was about 30 years older than his picture – at least 60, I'd say. The service was slow, and as we waited and waited he talked and talked about … himself.

I was told about all the beautiful young models who wanted him, and all the famous people he knew in the art and music industry. I was surprised that there was room at that table for me and his ego, truly.

At the end of the meal, he turned to me and said, 'You weren't nearly as boring as I thought you would be.' Harrumph! I had eaten well, so I smiled sweetly, said 'thank you very much', and walked out of the restaurant into the lovely rain.

## UNIT 11

Exercise 12, parts 1 and 2

### My kind of music

**A = Amy    M = Mum**

**A**  Mmmm, I like having the same name as Amy Winehouse. It was so sad when she died. She was only 27, and she had such a fabulous singing voice.

**M**  She did. It seems pop stars often die young. Look what happened to Brian Jones!

**A**  Who was he?

**M**  He was one of the Rolling Stones. He drowned in a swimming pool. That was years ago. He was 27, too.

**A**  Poor guy! Do you still like the Stones, mum?

**M**  Of course I do. They're my favourite group. They're still amazing after all these years.

**A**  Yeah – they're even older than you are.

**M**  Hey, they are all a lot older than me, but I've always loved them and their music. They've been singing together for nearly 50 years. Imagine that! I can't believe that any of the groups you like today will be together in 50 years' time.

**A**  Hmm! I can't begin to imagine anything 50 years from now. I'll be 65! Impossible!

**M**  I once thought like that. Not any more.

**A**  What were dad's favourite groups? Did he like the Stones?

**M**  No, he's never been a Stones fan. He didn't like the Beatles much either. In fact, your dad has never really liked pop music at all. He's more of a blues man. And jazz.

**A**  Yeah, I know. I hate the music he plays in the car when he takes me to school. It's all miserable blues stuff, you know, it kind of goes 'Oh, I'm so lonely, and life is soooo bad, and I can't find my socks in the morning. Oh miseryeeeee!'

**M**  Mmm, blues is a bit like that. It's the kind of music you either love or hate.

**A**  Well, I hate it. I like all kinds of music but not the blues.

**M**  Well, when you were very small we had to play your favourite children's songs all the time when we drove anywhere. If we put on any of our music, you just screamed. The same songs again and again. It drove us crazy!

**A**  Ooooh, I remember all those songs. Hey, it's good that I'm such a well-behaved child now, isn't it mum?

**M**  Well, I don't know about that.

**A**  Come on! Let's sing one those songs now.

It will cheer us up on a Monday morning. What was my favourite?

**M**  It was Old Macdonald had a farm – over and over and over again.

**A**  OK, then. Here we go, one two, three … 'Old Macdonald had a farm, e i e i oh! And on that farm he had a – er …

**M**  – er, a cow, e i e i oh

**M and A**  'With a moo, moo, here and a moo, moo there. Here a moo, there a moo, everywhere a moo, moo …'

## UNIT 12

Exercise 10, parts 1 and 2

### The meaning of dreams

**1 Robert**

I had a terrible dream – a nightmare really. I dreamt I was riding a horse, and I've never ridden a horse in my life, so that was strange. But anyway, I was riding this large brown horse, and I was being chased down the motorway by a police car with sirens blaring. Nee naw, nee naw! I knew if they caught me it would be the end, and I galloped faster and faster, and the horse was out of control and then … CRASH! I fell off into a field, and I woke up shouting 'Where's my horse?' And I could hear my wife saying, 'Robert, you've never had a horse! Go back to sleep!'

**2 Sonia**

I dreamt I was walking through this house. It was my house, but it wasn't my house, if you know what I mean. So … I went down the stairs, and I saw this door, and I thought 'That's funny. I don't remember that door in my house. Anyway, I opened it, and it was a room I'd never seen before, and the light in it was really bright, but it wasn't sunlight. And in my dream I thought 'this is really strange – a new room in my house.' I liked the room. It made me feel good, but I can't remember what it looked like.

**3 Harry**

I have this dream often. I'm back at school, and I have a really important exam. As I walk into the exam room, I realize that I haven't done any revision. In the dream I think maybe I'll be OK, I might know the answers, but when I turn over the paper nothing makes sense. Then I wake up with my heart pounding and think 'Thank goodness it was just a dream'.

**4 Lucy**

This is my favourite dream. I have it a lot. I dream that I can fly. I just push down on my legs and go up, up into the air – as high as I want. Every time I come down I just push up again, and when I'm up there I look down on the world below, and it looks beautiful. It is such a wonderful feeling. I can fly over towns and villages. In my dream I always say to myself, 'This is so amazing. Why don't I do it more often? Why doesn't everyone do it?' I feel so disappointed when I wake up and realize that I can't.

# Answer key

**1** 1 2 go  3 love  4 were born
5 moved  6 didn't like
7 'm taking  8 'm going to study

2 1 comes  2 's studying
3 'm enjoying  4 's going to work
5 has  6 likes  7 didn't start  8 gave

3 1 live  2 don't work  3 acts
4 prefer  5 went  6 made
7 didn't win  8 's doing

**2** 2 go  3 's surfing  4 works
5 'm going to work  6 's sitting
7 doesn't work  8 'm acting
9 are walking

**3** 2 a  3 c  4 c  5 a  6 c  7 a
8 a  9 a

**4** 2 Where *are* you going?
3 What language *is* she speaking?
4 What *are* you doing tonight?
5 Where *did* you buy your jeans?
6 What *are* you going to cook for
dinner?
7 How much money *does* he have?
8 *Did* you go to work yesterday?

**5** 2 is he going to make
3 do Jane and Peter live
4 Do they have
5 are you going
6 did you do/watch
7 was your grandmother born
8 did she get married

**6** 2 What  3 Where  4 Who
5 What  6 Why  7 What
8 When  9 Why

**7** 2 d  3 i  4 g  5 j  6 b  7 a
8 c  9 f  10 h

**8** 1 Who's  2 Whose  3 Whose
4 Who's  5 Who's  6 Whose

**9** 1 2 Do; make
3 tell; say
4 look; watch
5 borrow; lend

2 2 book, film  3 story, film
4 man, coffee  5 man, boy

3 2 at  3 for  4 at  5 of  6 in
7 with  8 for  9 to  10 of

4 2 rest, rest  3 flat, flat
4 kind, kind  5 left, left

**10** 1 2 Was it love at first sight?
3 Where did you go on your first date?
4 When and where did you get
married?
5 How many children do you have?
6 What does Andy do?
7 What do you like doing together?
8 Where are you going on your next
holiday?

2 1 No, she didn't.
2 She was immediately attracted to him.
3 They went to a gig.
4 Because it was very romantic.
5 They became proper grown-ups.
6 Because bands like recording in
sunny places.
7 Making music, playing with the
kids, and going to the cinema.
8 Cornwall.

**11** 1 1 He's getting married soon.
2 Love.
3 21.
4 Janice. Her friend.
5 Midnight.
6 Music.
7 Travel abroad with Andy on work
trips.
8 200.

2 1 getting  2 fell  3 know, mean
4 had, have  5 don't do
6 couldn't travel  7 having
8 enjoyed

**12** 1 2 foot  3 fun  4 cat  5 mean
6 work  7 win  8 walk

2 2 meat  3 four  4 son  5 board
6 peace

3 2 new  3 piece  4 bored  5 meat

**13** **In any order**
| | |
|---|---|
| good | could |
| food | rude |
| meal | feel |
| caught | sort |
| steak | make |
| saw | more |
| busy | fizzy |

**14** **Across**     **Down**
5 empty      1 quiet
6 last       2 late
10 wrong     4 terrible
11 boring    7 single
12 expensive 8 stupid
             9 worst

**1** 1 2 has  3 works  4 don't have
5 need  6 work  7 goes
8 don't feel  9 prefer  10 doesn't earn
11 doesn't matter  12 have

2 2 do Dave and his wife live
3 does he have  4 does he work
5 does he go  6 does he earn

3 2 don't go  3 doesn't like
4 don't earn, doesn't matter

4 2 No, he doesn't  3 Yes, he does
4 No, I don't  5 Yes, I do

**2** 2 do you think  3 don't understand
4 Do you need  5 belong  6 costs
7 doesn't matter  8 means  9 has
10 agree  11 Do you like  12 prefer

**3** 2 I usually have toast for breakfast.
3 I always watch TV in the morning.
4 How often do you have a holiday?
5 We sometimes go to a Japanese
restaurant.
6 I am never late for school.

**4** 2 works  3 enjoys  4 plays  5 goes
6 does  7 has  8 watches
9 finishes  10 relaxes  11 studies
12 tries

**5** 2 going  3 coming  4 having
5 taking  6 leaving  7 swimming
8 running  9 stopping
10 beginning  11 travelling  12 hitting

**6** 2 He works  3 Yes, he is.
4 She's an actress.  5 She works
6 No, she isn't.  7 She's playing tennis.

**7** 2 b  3 b  4 b  5 a  6 b  7 b  8 a

**8** 2 The sun *rises* in the east.
3 *I'm looking* for a white shirt in
medium. Have you got any?
4 'Where's Paul?' 'He's over there.
*He's talking* to Angela.'

5 She's 21 years old! *I don't believe* her!

6 I'm *learning* English for my job.

7 Why *are* you going out without a coat? It's freezing!

8 My father *works* in a bank.

**9** 1 1 happiness  2 before  3 worries
4 enough  5 aren't

2 1 Giving energy and time to close relationships.
2 Because a healthy body means a healthy mind.
3 Something you enjoy.
4 Go on holiday with people you love or have life-changing experiences.
5 Because the memory of these experiences stays with you forever.
6 Because he can't drive more than one car at the same time.
7 Friends and family.

**10** 1 **Ben, 8** his dog; he loves taking him for walks
**Kirstie, 10** Amy; she always laughs when she sees her, and her first word was her name
**Nigel, 41** when they all go walking in the countryside at the weekend; it makes him happy when they go for walks as a family, and he loves eating outdoors
**Fiona, 38** the first signs of spring, sunsets; she loves to see the trees turning green and the garden coming into life after winter, there's nothing more beautiful than glorious red sunset at the end of the day

2 2 nothing, dogs' (Ben)
3 laughs, holds, pick (Kirstie)
4 dirty, noisy, crowds (Nigel)
5 lots, don't cost (Fiona)
6 exciting (Fiona)
7 more, sunset (Fiona)
8 rude (Nigel)

**11** 1 2 going  3 Shopping  4 cooking
5 getting  6 Downloading
7 Making  8 Sending  9 chatting
10 doing  11 going  12 mending

2 2 driving licence
3 washing machine
4 shopping list
5 sleeping bag
6 swimming costume

**12** 1 2 has, 's got  3 has, 's got
4 have, 've got  5 have, 've got
6 has, 's got

2 1 Does, he does  2 Has, he has
3 Do, I don't  4 Do, they do
5 Have, they have  6 Have, I haven't

---

3 1 Have you got  2 've got
3 have you got  4 've got
5 haven't  6 Have you got
7 's got

4 2 I have a terrible headache
3 Do you have any aspirin?
4 You've got a beautiful flat!
5 Sally has a really good job.
6 I don't have any money.

**13**

| /s/ | /z/ | /ɪz/ |
|-----|-----|------|
| Pete's | Peters' | watches |
| wants | loves | relaxes |
| hates | runs | George's |
| Rick's | languages | pieces |
| tickets | Anna's | finishes |
| starts | teachers | |
| flats | rains | |
| clothes | Henry's | |
| | goes | |

**14** In any order
shopping, running, cooking, walking, sleeping, reading, swimming, drawing

**15**

| Across | Down |
|--------|------|
| 6 teeth | 2 sheep |
| 7 glasses | 3 boxes |
| 10 mice | 4 knives |
| 11 women | 5 children |
| 12 potatoes | 8 feet |
| | 9 toys |

**UNIT 3**

**1** 2 became  3 set off  4 reached
5 travelled  6 took  7 landed
8 controlled  9 planned  10 had
11 flew

**2** 1 2 did he have
3 did he set off
4 did he travel
5 did the journey take
6 did he land
7 did he have
8 was the first balloon crossing

2 2 He didn't set off from his garden. He set off from an airfield.
3 He didn't start his journey at 5.00 in the afternoon. He started it at 5.00 in the morning.
4 He didn't fly at 500 metres. He flew at 1,200 metres.
5 The journey wasn't 50 miles. It was 22 miles.

3 2 Yes, he did.  3 No, he didn't.
4 Yes, he did.  5 Yes, he did.

**3** 1 1 studied  tried  hurried
2 died  lived  arrived

---

3 planned  stopped  travelled
4 made  felt  sent  knew

2 2 ✓  3 ✗  4 ✗  5 ✗
6 ✓  7 ✗  8 ✗  9 ✗  10 ✓

**4** 1 2 in  3 at  4 in  5 on  6 at  7 at
8 in  9 in  10 at  11 in  12 at

2 2 *last* night  3 a week *ago*
4 ten years *ago*  5 *last* year
6 two months *ago*

3 2 on  3 in  4 ago  5 on  6 on
7 When  8 at  9 last  10 at

**5** 1 2 Penny was eating a cake.
3 Martin was drinking coffee.
4 Sally was shopping online.
5 Rob and Matt were talking about last night's match.

2 1 was Dave chatting
2 was Penny eating
3 were you buying
4 were you talking

3 2 weren't using  3 wasn't doing
4 weren't talking

**6** a 1, 5  b 3, 6  c 2, 4

**7** 3 was raining  4 rained
5 were you talking  6 talked
7 was wearing  8 did you wear
9 lived  10 was living

**8** 1 1 b  2 a  3 c  4 b  5 b

2 1 They laughed and shouted at him.
2 He said he was stopping the burglars.
3 The police.
4 She thought Paul and his girlfriend were moving furniture.
5 Because it was his own fault.

3 2 upside down  3 smashed
4 stuck  5 trapped  6 screaming
7 banging

**9** 1 the town  2 left  3 mobile phone
4 13, Close  5 brown, jeans
6 one o'clock  7 quite, grey
8 £50, house  9 didn't catch

**10** 1 1 father  2 thinks  3 wash  4 watch
5 Asian  6 just  7 English

2 /θ/ thirty
/ð/ weather, brother
/ʃ/ shop, station, sure
/ʒ/ measure, revision
/tʃ/ chocolate, catch, teacher
/dʒ/ danger, January
/ŋ/ drink, thing, wrong

**11** 2 Did you have a good time
3 have a word
4 had an argument
5 have a drink
6 had a shower

7 have a swim
8 have a break
9 had a dream

**12 In any order**
work hard, exercise regularly,
explain clearly, shine brightly,
wait patiently, forget completely

**13** Across    Down

| Across | | Down | |
|---|---|---|---|
| 4 | found | 1 | bought |
| 7 | thought | 2 | caught |
| 10 | fell | 4 | felt |
| 11 | wore | 5 | drove |
| 12 | gave | 6 | broke |
| 14 | stood | 8 | heard |
| 15 | forgot | 9 | flew |
| 16 | began | 13 | wrote |
| | | 14 | spoke |

## UNIT 4

**1** 2 butcher's  3 newsagent's
4 travel agent's  5 library
6 dry cleaner's  7 estate agent's
8 bookshop  9 hairdresser's

**2**

| Count nouns | Uncount nouns |
|---|---|
| stamp | petrol |
| car | meat |
| dollar | water |
| job | money |
| potato | rice |
| loaf | work |
| | fruit |
| | soup |
| | bread |
| | news |
| | information |

**3** 1 3 coffee  4 a coffee  5 glass
    6 a glass

  2 3 a cake  4 some cake
    5 a newspaper  6 some paper

**4** 1 1 any  2 any  3 some  4 any
    5 some  6 some  7 any  8 any
    9 some  10 some

  2 2 I don't want *any* rice.
    3 I'd like *some* information about
      hotels in the town, please.
    4 He has done *some* very good work
      recently.
    5 I haven't got *any* paper.
    6 Can I have *some* milk in my coffee,
      please?

**5** 1 How many  2 How much
    3 How many  4 How many
    5 How much  6 How many

**6** 3 many  4 much  5 a lot of, many
    6 much  7 a lot of  8 much

9 much  10 a lot of  11 much
12 a lot of

**7** 1 Just a little. I'm going to the dentist
    tomorrow.
  2 Just a few. I didn't know anyone.
  3 Just a little. I'm trying to lose weight.
  4 Just a few. You can borrow them if
    you like.

**8** 1 I help  2 'd like some
  3 How much are  4 Can I have
  5 have you got  6 Do you have
  7 Anything  8 all  9 How much
  10 That's

**9** 1 3 everything  4 nothing
    5 everywhere  6 somewhere
    7 No one 8 anyone  9 Everyone
    10 someone

  2 2 Nothing  3 anything  4 No one
    5 somewhere  6 Everyone

**10** 1 2 ✗ There are 10, 500 fish and chip
      shops in Britain.
    3 ✗ Joseph Malin's family fried chips
      in their home to sell.
    4 ✓
    5 ✓
    6 ✗ Charles Dickens wrote about
      fried fish.

  2 1 Because they believe a man called
    John Lees began selling fish and
    chips in a market in Mossley,
    Lancashire in 1863. .
    2 It is in honour of John Lees.
    3 More than 25,000.
    4 10,000.
    5 Burgers, kebabs, and pizzas.
    6 Paris, France.

  3 2 Joseph Malin
    3 Charles Dickens
    4 John Lees
    5 Harry Ramsden
    6 Oliver Dupart

**11** **Dave** his mum's roast dinner; on
a Sunday; his mum's are the best in
the world; roast beef, roast potatoes,
Yorkshire pudding, broccoli or peas,
gravy
**Sally** egg and tomato sandwiches;
when she goes for picnics in the
summer; she loves eating food
outdoors; chopped eggs, tomatoes,
mayonnaise, salt and pepper, white
sliced bread
**Freddie** hamburger and chips; two
or three times a week; because he
ate so many when he was a kid; a big
juicy burger, gherkins, salad, chips
with ketchup
**Lizzie** chicken curry; when she has

friends for supper; it doesn't taste like
the curries in Indian restaurants;
spices, garlic, tomato paste, yoghurt,
chicken, onions, potatoes, rice

**12** 1 2 the, a, the  3 a, a, the, a
    4 the, the  5 the, the
    6 a, the  7 the, the
    8 the, a, the, The

  2 1 Bees make honey.
    2 Children play with toys.
    3 Mechanics mend cars.
    4 Politicians tell lies.
    5 Butchers sell meat.
    6 Cats eat fish.

  3 2 Give Maria a ring. She's *at home*.
    3 I go to *school* by bus.
    4 My sister's *a* doctor.
    5 We have *the* best teacher in the
      world.
    6 I usually go *to bed* at midnight.

**13** 2 slice  3 can/bottle  4 bunch
    5 packet  6 bottle  7 piece
    8 can/bottle  9 bunch  10 packet
    11 packet/piece  12 bunch
    13 piece/slice  14 packet

**14**

| Vegetables | Fruit | Meat |
|---|---|---|
| courgette | lemon | turkey |
| pea | melon | ham |
| carrot | peach | beef |
| onion | raspberry | lamb |
| cauliflower | plum | |

**15** 1 2 Coke  3 pie  4 cow  5 toy
    6 beer  7 pear  8 more

  2 2 f  3 a  4 e  5 b  6 d
    7 h  8 g

**16 In any order**
salt and pepper
fish and chips
bread and butter
eggs and bacon
shirt and tie

**17** Across    Down

| Across | | Down | |
|---|---|---|---|
| 6 | clothes | 2 | sunglasses |
| 7 | stairs | 3 | tights |
| 8 | shorts | 4 | scissors |
| 9 | trousers | 5 | pyjamas |

## UNIT 5

**1** 2 to work  3 to do  4 learning
    5 thinking  6 to work  7 to go
    8 finding  9 to do/doing  10 to find
    11 to go  12 travelling
    13 driving  14 to cross

**2** 2 Sheila wants to be a teacher because
    she enjoys working with children.

**3** Mike would like to be a farmer because he likes working outside.

**4** James is going to work in IT because he wants to earn a lot of money.

**5** Jerry wants to be an accountant because he likes working with numbers.

**6** We're thinking of buying a cottage by the sea because we love sailing.

**3** 2 to earn   3 learning/to learn
4 to buy   5 learning   6 visiting
7 going   8 doing   9 stopping
10 to save

**4** 2 Do you like your teacher?
3 Do you like going to the cinema?
4 Would you like to go for a swim?
5 Would you like to go out tonight?

**5** 2 Would you like to see
3 like cooking
4 Would you like to borrow
5 Do you like watching

**6** 1 won't recognize   2 'll be
3 won't take   4 'll soon feel
5 won't be   6 'll see

**7** 2 I'll pay   3 I'll pick it up
4 I'll answer/get

**8** 2 It's going to rain.
3 He's going to learn Japanese.
4 They're going to play tennis.
5 She's going to water the plants.
6 She's going to miss the bus.

**9** 2 'm having, 're eating
3 are we having
4 're going
5 are you seeing, 'm having

**10** 2 b   3 b   4 a   5 b   6 a

**11** 2 2 want   3 chip   4 walk   5 won't
6 cheap   7 can't   8 fill   9 work
10 leave   11 live   12 fell   13 hit
14 hurt   15 full   16 can

**12** 1 2 medicine   3 dangerous
4 hard, passed
5 University College, London
6 citizen   7 paediatrician
8 International Red Cross

2 1 b   2 b   3 b   4 b   5 b   6 a
7 b   8 a

**13** 2 receive   3 arrive   4 become
5 earn   6 leave   7 arrive home

**14** 1 **Frankie Meazza, 17** he lived with his mum until she married again, he didn't get on with his stepdad so he left; he lives in a hostel, he's studying for his exams, he's learning to drive; he'd like to be a mechanic, he's thinking of joining the army

**Isabel Blair, 18** she was lazy, she just wanted to be with her friends and didn't do her schoolwork; she's got good exam results, she's doesn't know what she wants to study so she's going to give herself a year to think about it; she'd like to get work at her uncle's care home in Toronto

**James Owen, 17** his dad was ill; he's studying for his final school exams; he's going to Newcastle University to study medicine, he'd like to be a surgeon

2 2 James; 13
3 Frankie; Because he fought with his stepdad all the time.
4 Isabel; With her cousins in Canada.
5 James; Because the doctors and nurses who looked after his dad were so wonderful.
6 Frankie; Because you get good training in the army.

**15** 1 2 try   3 fill   4 get   5 look   6 Pick
7 look   8 run   9 give   10 look

2 2 down   3 up   4 down   5 back
6 round   7 out   8 out   9 out
10 away

**16** 

| Across | Down |
|---|---|
| 4 Iran | 1 Lebanon |
| 6 Argentina | 2 Wales |
| 9 Egypt | 5 Norway |
| 14 Ireland | 7 Poland |
| 15 Greece | 8 Slovakia |
| 16 Iraq | 10 Turkey |
| 17 Holland | 11 Chile |
| 18 Morocco | 12 Belgium |
|  | 13 Israel |

**17** 1 Egypt   2 Argentina
3 Holland   4 Greece

## UNIT 6

**1** 1 1 b, c   2 a, c   3 a, b   4 a, b   5 b, c

2 2 What's Pete like?
3 What does Pete like?
4 How's Pete?
5 Do you like Pete?

3 4, 6, 8

**2** 1 2 What's the food like?
3 What are the people like?
4 What's Sydney like?
5 What are the towns like?
6 What are the beaches like?

2 b 1   c 2   d 4   e 6   f 5

**3** 2 cheaper; the cheapest
3 bigger; the biggest
4 fatter; the fattest

5 hotter; the hottest
6 nicer; the nicest
7 safer; the safest
8 easier; the easiest
9 noisier; the noisiest
10 happier; the happiest
11 more expensive; the most expensive
12 more difficult; the most difficult
13 more intelligent; the most intelligent
14 more modern; the most modern
15 more handsome; the most handsome
16 better; best
17 worse; the worst
18 further; the furthest

**4** 2 Matt, Nellie
3 happier
4 Nellie, than Matt
5 Nellie, than Matt
6 more interesting job than Matt
7 Nellie's house, than Matt's
8 more expensive than Matt's
9 more, than Nellie's

**5** 2 No, she didn't. She bought the most expensive.
3 No, it isn't. It's the most difficult.
4 No, you aren't. You're the laziest.
5 No, he isn't. He's the most generous.
6 No, it isn't. It's the worst.

**6** 2 as hot as   3 as good as
4 not as tall as   5 as intelligent as
6 as well as

**7** 1 It's the biggest in the world.
2 Yours is the same as mine.
3 She's older then her brothers.
4 I look like my mother.
5 They're different from the others.

**8** 1 1 the most popular   2 the tallest
3 the best   4 the biggest   5 best
6 the biggest   7 the most beautiful

2 1 135   2 40   3 30
4 £16.00, £8.50   5 2,200   6 30,000

3 1 Regent's Park
2 The British museum
3 The London Eye
4 The London Eye
5 Regent's Park
6 Regent's Park

**9** 1 The London Eye, Buckingham Palace, Westminster Abbey, Picadilly Circus, Big Ben, Hyde Park, Trafalgar Square

2 1 upstairs   2 Piccadilly Circus
3 smaller   4 as big as   5 wasn't
6 eleven   7 year   8 Hyde

**10** 1 2 e   3 a   4 b   5 d   6 g   7 i
8 f   9 h   10 g

2 2 good-looking   3 terrible
4 clever   5 huge   6 annoyed

**3** 2 impolite   3 inexpensive
   4 unhappy   5 uninteresting
   6 incorrect   7 unintelligent
   8 impossible

**4** 2 messy   3 cheap   4 miserable
   5 boring   6 wrong   7 stupid
   8 kind

**5** 1 cheap   2 tidy   3 boring
   4 right   5 kind   6 miserable
   7 stupid   8 polite

**11**

| ● ● ● | ● ● ● | ● ● ● |
|---|---|---|
| interesting | ambitious | magazine |
| difficult | expensive | afternoon |
| sociable | successful | understand |
| wonderful | apartment | |
| customer | surprising | |
| yesterday | religious | |
| Mexican | important | |
| | delicious | |

**12**   2 e   3 f   4 c   5 d   6 b

**13**

| People | Places |
|---|---|
| cheerful | historic |
| kind | cosy |
| warm | exciting |
| lazy | modern |
| selfish | touristy |
| shy | crowded |

| Colours | The weather |
|---|---|
| white | showery |
| grey | foggy |
| purple | warm |
| brown | sunny |
| black | windy |
| orange | wet |

### UNIT 7

**1** 1 2 's travelled.   3 's met   4 've played
   5 's climbed   6 's crossed   7 's seen
   8 's written   9 's won   10 's been
   11 've lived   12 've had

   2 2 've travelled   3 've never lost
   4 've been   5 've lived

**2** 1 1 have you worked
   2 have you met
   3 Have you ever played
   4 have you written
   5 have you been

   2 2 The US president hasn't beaten
   him at golf.
   3 He and his wife haven't moved
   house for a long time.

   4 He hasn't lived in a better place
   than Long Island.

   3 2 No, he hasn't   3 Yes, they have
   4 No, they haven't   5 Yes, he has

**3** 2 saw; seen   3 wrote; written
   4 won: won   5 came; come
   6 went; gone   7 was; been
   8 had; had   9 read; read
   10 did; done   11 began; begun
   12 found; found   13 ate, eaten

**4** 1 1 for   2 since   3 for   4 for   5 since

   2 1 b   2 a   3 b   4 b   5 a   6 a

**5** 1 2 arrived here at six o'clock
   3 bought it last week
   4 wrote it two years ago
   5 went there in 2008
   6 started it on 17 July
   7 lost it last night
   8 worked as a waiter for two months
   9 lived there when I was a student
   10 had a curry before we left home

   2 at six o'clock, last week, two years ago,
   in 2008, on 17 July, last night, when I
   was a student, before we left home

**6** 1 1 have you ever lived   2 had
   3 've never lived   4 haven't even cooked
   5 Did you like

   2 1 have you had   2 haven't seen
   3 've had   4 did you get
   5 did you pay

   3 1 've known   2 did you meet
   3 met   4 went   5 's worked

**7** 2 No, thanks. I've seen it *already*./
   No, thanks. I've *already* seen it.
   3 I haven't washed it *yet*. Sorry.
   4 I don't know. I've *never* been there.
   5 The postman hasn't been *yet*. He
   doesn't come till later.
   6 I've *just* spoken to him. He knows all
   about it./I've spoken to him *already*.
   He knows all about it./I've *already*
   spoken to him. He knows all about it.

**8** 2 haven't eaten   3 haven't read
   4 've never eaten   5 've already had
   6 've only just taken

**9** 2 c   3 a   4 b   5 a   6 a

**10** 1 2 Yes, he is.
   3 A Honda 125 cc
   4 It started in Veracruz on the Gulf of
   Mexico and ended in Pennsylvania
   5 Six months.
   6 India.

   2 2 He hasn't ridden a motorbike for
   *40* years.
   3 The journey was *14,000* miles long.

   4 He was kidnapped for *a short time*
   in *Venezuela*.
   5 He broke his *leg* in Chile.
   6 He paid *$9* for a hotel room in
   Bolivia.
   7 He hopes to be in *India* for his
   77th birthday.
   8 He's *been* to India *before*.

**11** 1 2 S   3 S   4 E & N   5 E & N
   6 S   7 S   8 E & N

   2 1 goes so fast
   2 We've always been
   3 argue about anything
   4 did you two meet
   5 always lived around

   3 1 died two years ago, 've been on
   2 met at school, both 16
   3 trying, its ups and downs
   4 Did, have
   5 've moved to a

**13** 1 2 politician; political
   3 artist; artistic
   4 musician; musical
   5 chemist; chemical
   6 scientist; scientific
   7 economist; economic
   8 photographer; photographic

   2 2 chemical   3 scientist   4 musical
   5 politician   6 history
   7 economic   8 photographic

   3 2 ambitious   3 success
   4 health   5 fashionable
   6 noise   7 comfortable
   8 popularity

**14**

| Across | Down |
|---|---|
| 5 cousins | 1 refugee |
| 7 lawyers | 3 thief |
| 8 minister | 4 politician |
| 10 widow | 6 soldier |
| 11 farmer | 9 immigrant |
| 13 foreigner | 12 terrorist |
| 15 ancestors | 14 guide |
| 17 passenger | 16 fan |

### UNIT 8

**1** 1 2 have to play   3 do you have to do
   4 do you have to run   5 has to run
   6 has to be   7 don't have to go
   8 have to watch   9 doesn't have to watch

   2 2 do the players have to
   3 does Tony have to
   4 do footballers have to
   5 Does Tony's wife have to

**2** 1 3 O   4 P   5 P   6 O   7 O   8 P

**3** 1 Did you have to
   2 had to
   3 did your brother have to

4 had to
5 Did children have to
6 did you have to
7 didn't have to

**4** **Students' own answers**

**5** 2 *Do you have to* wear a uniform in your job?
3 I *have to* study very hard because I want to get a good job.
4 We *don't have to* get up early tomorrow. It's Saturday!
5 When I was a child I *had* to help my mother with the housework.
6 *Do you have* an English lesson today?

**6** 1 2 I think he should go by bus instead.
3 I think you should go to the dentist.
4 I don't think they should get married.
5 I think you should feed her.
6 I don't think you should eat so much cake.
7 I think you should take them back to the shop.

2 2 do you think we should go
3 do you think I should do
4 do you think we should invite
5 do you think I should cook

**7** 2 have to   3 have to   4 should
5 should   6 has to   7 should
8 Do we have to   9 should
10 have to

**8** 2 must tidy   3 must meet
4 must call   5 must look after
6 must go   7 must write

**9** 1 1 mustn't   2 don't have to
3 don't have to   4 mustn't
5 mustn't   6 don't have to
7 doesn't have to   8 mustn't

**10** 1 2 licence, 2   3 150, commercial
4 6, logs   5 12, day   6 6, off

2 2 ✗ Military pilots don't have to pay for their lessons.
3 ✓
4 ✗ She had to carry huge logs from the forest to trucks in Wisconsin.
5 ✗ She now works as a rescue pilot.
6 ✓
7 ✗ The students at her school come from all over the world.
8 ✓
9 ✗ She thinks there should be more scholarships for women pilots.

**11** 1 For over four years.
2 About £37,000 a year without Sundays. If she works Sundays, she gets paid more.
3 She loves trains. The best part is the kids who wave from bridges as she goes past.

4 The hours. She has to work a 35 hour week but at different times. Sometimes she starts at two in the morning, but on other days she starts at eleven at night.
5 She was a shop manager at a clothes shop, but she hated it. A friend's wife who worked for the railway said she should try it, and she took a job as a ticket inspector. After six months she took the exam to be a train driver.
6 TV stars and lots of politicians.
7 Yes – it's awful.
8 It's OK. Most drivers are men, but they're good friends. They sometimes make fun of her.
9 Go for it, if you are interested. It's exciting but not glamorous – you'll probably hate the uniform. It's a great job, and the money isn't bad.

**12** 1

| make | do |
|---|---|
| a cake | the housework |
| a phone call | my homework |
| up my mind | the shopping |
| a noise | an IT course |
| | your best |
| | the washing-up |
| | me a favour |

2 2 make a cake
3 make up my mind
4 do your best
5 do me a favour
6 make friends
7 do the shopping
8 make a phone call

3

| take | put |
|---|---|
| a photo | some music on |
| my advice | your glasses on |
| a long time | the date in my diary |
| the children to the zoo | suncream on |
| your coat off | |

4 1 taking the children to the zoo
2 take a photo
3 put your glasses on
4 put the date in my diary
5 takes a long time
6 put some music on
7 take my advice
8 put suncream on

**13** 1 2 a   3 c   4 a   5 a   6 c
7 b   8 c   9 b

2 2 d   3 f   4 e   5 a   6 i
7 h   8 b   9 g

**3** 1 short   fourth
2 hurt   world
3 fruit   through
4 mine   height
5 slow   joke

**14** Across       Down
3 skirt       2 shorts
6 belt        4 tie
9 suit        5 socks
11 jacket     6 boots
12 cap        7 gloves
13 scarf      8 pyjamas
14 jumper     10 trainers
15 sandals

**UNIT 9**

**1** 1 3 ran   4 had eaten   5 appeared
6 had brought   7 had heard
8 led   9 drowned   10 had been
11 left   12 had done

2 1 had never been   2 had seen
3 had promised   4 had disappeared
5 hadn't paid

**2** 1 1 I was hungry because I hadn't eaten anything all day.
2 I was tired because I hadn't slept well the night before.
3 I didn't have any money because I'd spent it all on clothes.
4 I was late for work because I hadn't set my alarm clock.
5 My mother was worried because I hadn't been in touch for a week.
6 My father was angry because I'd crashed his car.

2 3 went   4 'd gone   5 gave
6 'd given

**3** (present) He'd killed the evil villain, Professor Zaros. He'd flown to the Mexican desert. He'd got up early.

**4** 1 2 d   3 e   4 c   5 f   6 a

2 2 After the guests had gone home, I tidied up./I tidied up after the guests had gone home.
3 Although he'd earned a lot of money in his life, he died a poor man.
4 Before I'd left the house, she woke up./She woke up before I'd left the house.
5 We didn't stop cleaning until we'd done every room in the house.
6 As soon as I'd written my essay, I went to bed./I went to bed as soon as I'd written my essay.
7 I'd been very rude to him, so I rang and apologized.
8 I ran to the station, but the train had already gone.

**5** 2 or   3 When   4 but
5 because   6 While   7 until

**6 2** 1 ring, ring   2 fan, fan
3 waves, Wave   4 type, types
5 boots, boot

**3** 2 Fine, fine   3 lie, lie   4 mean, mean
5 play, play   6 match, match
7 fair, fair   8 flat, flat

**7** 1 Yes, she does.
2 In London.
3 For his dad's 70th birthday.
4 For her sister's wedding.
5 He studied Law instead.
6 He's a lawyer. No, he doesn't.
7 Paint.
8 Amanda left Peter.
9 They were too young.

**8** 1 15 years.
2 18.
3 They sat together by the river on a perfect sunny afternoon.
4 He'd treated his mother badly.
5 Younger.
6 Café Bella. Yes, they'd been there before.
7 No, he doesn't.
8 Because he seemed to have no regrets.

**9** 2 was looking, spoke
3 'd spent, had told, loved
4 had left, wanted
5 'd come
6 felt, had treated
7 was wearing, wore
8 had missed, didn't say
9 didn't arrange

**10** 1

| /iː/ | /e/ |
|---|---|
| team | bread |
| mean | health |
| read (present) | read (past) |
| bean | head |
| /ɪə/ | /eə/ |
| fear | bear |
| year | pear |
| /eɪ/ | /ɜː/ |
| great | earth |
| steak | earn |

2 3 ✓   4 ✗   5 ✓   6 ✗   7 ✗   8 ✗
9 ✗   10 ✓   11 ✗   12 ✗

**11** 1 2 Alice   3 Henry   4 Jane and John
5 me   6 Sally   7 Pat and Paul

**12** **Across**
4 mend
6 push
8 borrow
10 lose
11 finish
12 catch
14 remember

**Down**
3 import
5 drop
7 save
9 whisper
10 leave
11 fail
13 cry

## UNIT 10

**1 1** 1 1 has been developed   2 are used
3 were developed
4 be produced   5 will be used

1 2 1 were injured   2 were taken
3 was killed   4 was hit
5 will be closed

2 1 b   2 a   3 b   4 b

**2** **Present Simple**
2 is insured   3 are watched
4 is the post delivered   5 're covered
6 is kept   7 are killed
**Past Simple**
2 Was your car damaged   3 was sold
4 was introduced   5 was locked
6 were taken
**Present Perfect**
2 Have you ever been questioned
3 've been sacked   4 's been delayed
5 has just been promoted
***Will***
2 will be sent
3 will the next Olympic Games be held

**3** 2 Where is Hindi spoken?
In India.
3 How many people were killed in the Second World War?
Between 60 and 80 million people.
4 Where were the Olympic Games held in 2008?
In China.
5 How many iPhones have been made?
More than 100 million!

**4** 2 No it isn't! It's made in France.
3 No they aren't. They are made by Apple.
4 No it wasn't! It was painted by Leonardo Da Vinci.
5 No they weren't! They were built in Egypt.

**5** 2 be spent   3 be served
4 be cleaned   5 be banned
6 be taken   7 be knocked down
8 be cancelled   9 be contacted

**6 1** 2 a   3 a   4 b   5 a   6 b

2 1 grew up   2 was educated
3 studied   4 be used
5 was shown   6 invested
7 were manufactured

8 have been sold   9 has been given
10 started   11 is based

**7 1** 2 Charlotte's husband and Zoe and Will's father
3 Charlotte's husband, Rose's father, and Zoe and Will's stepfather
4 daughter   5 son   6 daughter

2 1 Charlotte   2 Guy   3 Zoe and Rose
4 Fred

3 1 He was killed in an aircrash.
2 A photographic business.
3 A 'daddy shop'.
4 A daddy with a nice smile and kind eyes.
5 No, she didn't.
6 Because she knew he wasn't happy being alone.
7 The engagement ring.
8 The three children. It told the story of how Charlotte and Guy had met.

**8 1** 1 He was better looking than his photograph.
2 They didn't talk about anything.
3 He told her that he loved Vivaldi and the classics.
4 Her sister.
5 A pair of shorts, tennis shoes and a football shirt, and a baseball cap turned backwards.
6 He showed her some pictures of his wife and family.
7 His cousin.
8 Because she was a Scorpio and he was a Gemini.
9 His cousin.
10 Any information about Michael.
11 About 60.
12 All the beautiful young models who wanted him, and all the famous people he knew in the art and music industry.

2 1 S   2 A   3 C   4 M   5 C
6 M   7 S

3 1 Because her date wasn't as good as she expected.
2 Because everything about the meeting was bad. He didn't look like the person in the photo, and he and a wife and children.
3 Because his date didn't think they should go out together because of their star signs.
4 Because he talked and talked about himself.

**9** 2 determined   3 shocked
4 disappointed   5 surprised
6 horrified   7 annoyed   8 amused
9 talented   10 delighted

**10** 1  2 head  3 star  4 coffee  5 ticket
6 hair  7 station  8 sun  9 book
10 traffic

2  2 hairdresser  3 sunset
4 traffic jam  5 traffic lights
6 fireman  7 sunglasses
8 headphones

3  2 in a cook book  3 the postman
4 a parking ticket  5 suncream
6 the sunset  7 your head lights
8 a petrol station

**11** 2  2 listen  3 climb  4 island
5 foreign  6 farm  7 walk
8 wrong  9 autumn  10 could
11 sandwich  12 daughter

3  2 farm  3 island  4 could
5 climb  6 autumn  7 foreign
8 listen  9 sandwich

**12** Across                     Down
4 newsagent's          2 butcher's
5 toy shop               3 travel agent's
7 jeweller's             6 chemist's
8 book shop             9 baker's
10 hairdresser's

UNIT 11

**1** 1  1 haven't heard  2 Have you started
3 spoke  4 didn't know
5 gave  6 have gone
7 've bought  8 found
9 Have you seen  10 haven't seen

2  1 have been  2 Have you ever been
3 arrived  4 remembered  5 started
6 've made  7 've been
8 haven't seen  9 knew

**2** 1 did Paul last speak
2 has he just bought
3 did he find
4 did he last see
5 has Sally been
6 Has she started
7 Has she seen
8 have Helen and Rafael known

**3** 1 gone  2 been, been  3 gone
4 gone  5 been  6 been

**4** 2 have been playing
3 has been studying
4 've been learning
5 've been looking
6 've been trying
7 've been watching
8 's been revising

**5** 1 Have you been waiting
2 have you been playing
3 Has it been raining
4 have the children been doing
5 has he been going out

6 Have you been watching

**6** 2 f  3 a  4 b  5 h  6 d
7 e  8 g

**7** 2 a  3 b  4 a  5 a  6 b
7 b  8 a

**8** 1  1 've been learning  2 like
3 've been  4 went  5 stayed
6 have never seen  7 spent

2  1 's been trying  2 left
3 's had  4 's been working
5 wants  6 's written
7 's had

**9** 2 trained  3 have you made
4 Have you ever won
5 did your parents do
6 got  7 was running
8 do you do  9 'm shooting
10 've ever read  11 's ever said
12 Do you prefer  13 did you last cry
14 've ever made

**10** 1  2 tidy  3 set  4 take  5 pick
6 give  7 Slow

2  2 back  3 up  4 away  5 off
6 out  7 up  8 out

**11** 1  3, 4, 6, 7

2  2 ✓
3 ✗ They wanted a 'bad-boy' image
in contrast to the Beatles.
4 ✓
5 ✗ Ronnie Wood joined the band
five years after Brian Jones died.
6 ✓
7 ✗ Only Mick Jagger has been
knighted.
8 ✗ They played in St Petersburg in
2007.

3  2 Charlie Watts
3 The Beatles
4 Brian Jones
5 Mick Jagger
6 Keith Richards
7 Queen Elizabeth II, Mick Jagger
8 50,000 fans

**12** 1  1 The Rolling Stones.
2 Blues and jazz.
3 She likes all kinds of music. She
doesn't like blues.
4 Monday.

2  1 27  2 lot  3 can't  4 15
5 wasn't  6 makes fun of
7 screamed

**13** 1  2 bean  3 no  4 wear  5 here
6 weight  7 court  8 peace

2  1 wood  2 blue  3 week
4 threw  5 road  6 nose
7 buy  8 saw

3  1 sore, been, week
2 weight, piece
3 blue, Where, buy
4 rode, road
5 through, wood
6 threw, caught

**14** Across                 Down
3 singer              2 musicians
6 dancer             4 songwriter
8 actress            5 artist
9 actor               7 composer
11 drummer        10 poet
12 novelist
13 playwright

UNIT 12

**1** 2 enjoy fine food  3 'll enjoy
4 'll want to go on  5 book
6 'll put  7 'll give

**2** 1  2 What will you do if your plane is
delayed?
3 What will you do if the hotels are
full?
4 What will you do if you don't like
the food?
5 What will you do if you get
sunburnt?
6 Where will you go if the beaches
are crowded?

2  a 4  b 5  c 1  d 3  e 2  f 6

**3** 1  1 If  2 when  3 when  4 If
5 If  6 when  7 If

2  A Bye, darling! Have a good trip!
B Thanks. I'll call you when I arrive at
the hotel.
A But I'm going out tonight.
Remember?
B Well, *if* you*'re* out when I call, *I'll
leave* a message on the answer phone.
A Great. What time do you think
you'll be there?
B *If* the plane *arrives* on time, *I'll* be at
the hotel about 10.00 in the evening
your time.
A OK. I hope everything goes well. Let
me know *when* you have the time of
your flight home, and I*'ll pick* you up
at the airport.
B Right! Have a nice time *while* I*'m*
away! Don't miss me too much!

**4** 2 We might go to Spain on holiday.
3 I might go out tonight.
4 Jane might invite me to her party.
5 I might get some money for my
birthday.

**5** 1 might
2 might go out, might stay in
3 'll see

4 might make
5 'm taking
6 are going to get married

**6** 1 2 'd get up   3 'd drive
4 wouldn't work   5 'd go   6 'd wear

2 2 When/What time would he get up?
3 What kind of car would he drive?
4 How many hours a day would he work?
5 Where would he go on holiday?
6 What would he wear?

**7** 2 had, 'd go
3 had, 'd grow
4 had, 'd take up

**8** 1 1 were, 'd travel
2 see, 'll tell
3 'll come, like
4 came, 'd understand
5 were, 'd be

2 1 would you do, won
2 were, 'd join
3 'd go, was
4 'd buy, were
5 is, 'll go
6 spoke, wouldn't have to

**9** 1 1 Why we need sleep. If we didn't sleep, we'd die.
2 About a third.
3 Sleep.
4 They both took naps.
5 Because she woke him up.

2 1 three
2 body, brain
3 from lack of sleep
4 four
5 disc jockey, eight
6 Sancho Panza

3 1 Wise Men of Greece.
2 Percentage of deeper sleep
3 The year Michael Corke died.
4 The year King Perseus was killed,
5 The number of hours Peter Tripp stayed awake.
6 The number of years Epimenides the Wise slept for.

**10** 1 1 a horse   2 a house
3 school   4 flying

2 1 police, motorway   2 horse, sleep
3 door   4 room, sunlight
5 revision   6 heart
7 legs, air   8 feeling, world

**11** **Verb + preposition**
2 for   3 to   4 with   5 for   6 of
**Preposition + noun**
2 on   3 by   4 at   5 In   6 on

**Adjective + preposition**
1 in   2 with   3 about   4 of
5 of   6 about
**Noun + preposition**
1 for   2 with   3 of   4 to
5 of   6 on

**12** 1

| ● • • | • ● • | • • ● |
|---|---|---|
| envelope | advantage | understand |
| president | decision | entertain |
| universe | ambitious | |
| accident | direction | |
| passionate | forever | |
| happiness | remember | |
| | musician | |

| ● • | • ● |
|---|---|
| wallet | agree |
| system | award |
| ocean | reply |
| business | divorced |
| practice | become |
| programme | |
| different | |

**13** **Across**
2 stayed
4 friendly
7 forward
8 while
9 looked
12 carefully
16 international
17 important
18 been

**Down**
1 learning
3 sunbathe
5 learned
6 palace
10 online
11 getting
13 going
14 make
15 ago

# Irregular verbs

| Base form | Past Simple | Past participle | Base form | Past Simple | Past participle |
|---|---|---|---|---|---|
| be | was/were | been | leave | left | left |
| beat | beat | beaten | lend | lent | lent |
| become | became | become | let | let | let |
| begin | began | begun | lie | lay | lain |
| bend | bent | bent | light | lighted/lit | lighted/lit |
| bite | bit | bitten | lose | lost | lost |
| blow | blew | blown | make | made | made |
| break | broke | broken | mean | meant | meant |
| bring | brought | brought | meet | met | met |
| build | built | built | must | had to | had to |
| buy | bought | bought | pay | paid | paid |
| can | could | been able | put | put | put |
| catch | caught | caught | read /ri:d/ | read /red/ | read /red/ |
| choose | chose | chosen | ride | rode | ridden |
| come | came | come | ring | rang | rung |
| cost | cost | cost | rise | rose | risen |
| cut | cut | cut | run | ran | run |
| dig | dug | dug | say | said | said |
| do | did | done | see | saw | seen |
| draw | drew | drawn | sell | sold | sold |
| dream | dreamed/dreamt | dreamed/dreamt | send | sent | sent |
| drink | drank | drunk | set | set | set |
| drive | drove | driven | shake | shook | shaken |
| eat | ate | eaten | shine | shone | shone |
| fall | fell | fallen | shoot | shot | shot |
| feed | fed | fed | show | showed | shown |
| feel | felt | felt | shut | shut | shut |
| fight | fought | fought | sing | sang | sung |
| find | found | found | sink | sank | sunk |
| fit | fit | fit | sit | sat | sat |
| fly | flew | flown | sleep | slept | slept |
| forget | forgot | forgotten | slide | slid | slid |
| forgive | forgave | forgiven | speak | spoke | spoken |
| freeze | froze | frozen | spend | spent | spent |
| get | got | got | spoil | spoiled/spoilt | spoiled/spoilt |
| give | gave | given | spread | spread | spread |
| go | went | been/gone | stand | stood | stood |
| grow | grew | grown | steal | stole | stolen |
| hang | hanged/hung | hanged/hung | stick | stuck | stuck |
| have | had | had | swim | swam | swum |
| hear | heard | heard | take | took | taken |
| hide | hid | hidden | teach | taught | taught |
| hit | hit | hit | tear | tore | torn |
| hold | held | held | tell | told | told |
| hurt | hurt | hurt | think | thought | thought |
| keep | kept | kept | throw | threw | thrown |
| kneel | knelt | knelt | understand | understood | understood |
| know | knew | known | wake | woke | woken |
| lay | laid | laid | wear | wore | worn |
| lead | led | led | win | won | won |
| learn | learned/learnt | learned/learnt | write | wrote | written |

# Phonetic symbols

| Consonants | | | |
|---|---|---|---|
| 1 | /p/ | as in | **pen** /pen/ |
| 2 | /b/ | as in | **big** /bɪg/ |
| 3 | /t/ | as in | **tea** /tiː/ |
| 4 | /d/ | as in | **do** /duː/ |
| 5 | /k/ | as in | **cat** /kæt/ |
| 6 | /g/ | as in | **go** /gəʊ/ |
| 7 | /f/ | as in | **four** /fɔː/ |
| 8 | /v/ | as in | **very** /ˈveri/ |
| 9 | /s/ | as in | **son** /sʌn/ |
| 10 | /z/ | as in | **zoo** /zuː/ |
| 11 | /l/ | as in | **live** /lɪv/ |
| 12 | /m/ | as in | **my** /maɪ/ |
| 13 | /n/ | as in | **near** /nɪə/ |
| 14 | /h/ | as in | **happy** /ˈhæpi/ |
| 15 | /r/ | as in | **red** /red/ |
| 16 | /j/ | as in | **yes** /jes/ |
| 17 | /w/ | as in | **want** /wɒnt/ |
| 18 | /θ/ | as in | **thanks** /θæŋks/ |
| 19 | /ð/ | as in | **the** /ðə/ |
| 20 | /ʃ/ | as in | **she** /ʃiː/ |
| 21 | /ʒ/ | as in | **television** /ˈtelɪvɪʒn/ |
| 22 | /tʃ/ | as in | **child** /tʃaɪld/ |
| 23 | /dʒ/ | as in | **German** /ˈdʒɜːmən/ |
| 24 | /ŋ/ | as in | **English** /ˈɪŋglɪʃ/ |

| Vowels | | | |
|---|---|---|---|
| 25 | /iː/ | as in | **see** /siː/ |
| 26 | /ɪ/ | as in | **his** /hɪz/ |
| 27 | /i/ | as in | **twenty** /ˈtwenti/ |
| 28 | /e/ | as in | **ten** /ten/ |
| 29 | /æ/ | as in | **stamp** /stæmp/ |
| 30 | /ɑː/ | as in | **father** /ˈfɑːðə/ |
| 31 | /ɒ/ | as in | **hot** /hɒt/ |
| 32 | /ɔː/ | as in | **morning** /ˈmɔːnɪŋ/ |
| 33 | /ʊ/ | as in | **football** /ˈfʊtbɔːl/ |
| 34 | /uː/ | as in | **you** /juː/ |
| 35 | /ʌ/ | as in | **sun** /sʌn/ |
| 36 | /ɜː/ | as in | **learn** /lɜːn/ |
| 37 | /ə/ | as in | **letter** /ˈletə/ |

| Diphthongs (two vowels together) | | | |
|---|---|---|---|
| 38 | /eɪ/ | as in | **name** /neɪm/ |
| 39 | /əʊ/ | as in | **no** /nəʊ/ |
| 40 | /aɪ/ | as in | **my** /maɪ/ |
| 41 | /aʊ/ | as in | **how** /haʊ/ |
| 42 | /ɔɪ/ | as in | **boy** /bɔɪ/ |
| 43 | /ɪə/ | as in | **hear** /hɪə/ |
| 44 | /eə/ | as in | **where** /weə/ |
| 45 | /ʊə/ | as in | **tour** /tʊə/ |

# Notes

**OXFORD**
UNIVERSITY PRESS

Great Clarendon Street, Oxford, OX2 6DP, United Kingdom

Oxford University Press is a department of the University of Oxford.
It furthers the University's objective of excellence in research, scholarship,
and education by publishing worldwide. Oxford is a registered trade
mark of Oxford University Press in the UK and in certain other countries

ISBN: 978 0 19 476959 4     Book
ISBN: 978 0 19 476964 8     Book and iChecker Pack
ISBN: 978 0 19 477018 7     iChecker

Printed in China

This book is printed on paper from certified and well-managed sources

ACKNOWLEDGEMENTS

*Commissioned photography by*: Gareth Boden pp.6, 8 & 9

*Illustrations by*: Ian Baker pp.12, 23, 34 (Ex 7), 55; Fausto Bianchi/Beehive
p.60; Gill Button pp.7, 19, 24, 27 (Ex 8), 31, 33, 34 (Ex 8), 44, 52, 59, 62, 71,
80, 83; Simon Cooper/The Organisation pp.5, 17, 20, 26, 27 (Ex 6), 56, 58, 63,
66, 73; Tom Croft p.57; Lucy Davey/The Artworks p.30, 42; Maxwell Dorsey/
Meiklejohn Illustration Ltd pp.41, 75; Penko Gelev p.61; Ned Jolliffe p.25;
Gavin Reece p.16

*We would also like to thank the following for permission to reproduce the following
photographs*: Alamy pp.4 (Miguel/Ken Weingart), 20 (present/Timothy Hodgkinson),
21 (pensioner/paul abbitt rf), 21 (coins/PjrStudio), 29 (fish and chips/Simon
Price), 36 (Cambridge college/Eric Nathan), 43 (Lightworks Media), 43 (The
London Eye/Peter Barritt), 43 (Hyde Park/Robert Preston Photography),
43 (Madame Tussaud's/Alex Segre), 43 (The British Museum/Walter Bibikow/
Jon Arnold Images Ltd), 43 (Regent's Park/Steve Vidler/ImageState), 72 (petrol
station/Ben Molyneux Retail), 72 (hairdresser/Marco Baass/fStop), 72 (sunset/BL
Images Ltd), 72 (sunglasses/D. Hurst), 83 (car/Stephen Dorey), 85 (Thomas Edison/
Chris Hellier); Camera Press, London p.69 (Justin G. Thomas ); The Bridgeman
Art Library p.85 Sir Edward Burne-Jones, *The Sleeping Princess*, 1874, oil on canvas,
Dublin City Gallery, The Hugh Lane, Ireland; Corbis pp.4 (Lisbet/Ben Welsh/
Design Pics), 4 (Tom and Fay/Simon Potter/cultura), 13 (Tom/Mango Productions/
Ivy), 21 (channel champion/Ashley Jouhar/cultura), 29 (Dave/A. Inden/Flirt),
29 (Sally/Mario Castello/Fancy), 29 (Freddie/Patrick Lane/Somos Images),
29 (Lizzie/HBSS/Fancy), 35 (work/Tetra Images), 38 (Istanbul/Murat Taner/
Bridge), 38 (Amsterdam/Image Source), 38 (Athens/Ocean), 43 (Buckingham
Palace/Sylvain Sonnet/Terra), 43 (Big Ben/Ocean), 43 (St Paul's Cathedral/Rudy
Sulgan/Terra), 51 (couple/Peter Beck/Surf), 56 ( Newmann/zefa), 64 (Sonntag/
beyond/Alloy), 65 (Patrick Lane/Fancy), 72 (fireman/Bill Stormont/Flirt),
76 (Florence/Atlantide Phototravel/Terra), 81 ( Eberhard Streichan/zefa),
84 (Margaret Thatcher/Bettmann); Laura Crook p.22; www.simongandolfi.com
p.50; Getty Images pp.11 (sheep farmer/Chris Wahlberg/Workbook Stock),
13 (Laura/Jupiterimages/Workbook Stock), 14 (family mountain walking/Ben
Meyer/Cultura), 14 (montage/Paul Viant/The Image Bank), 15 (family/ULTRA.F/
Photodisc), 15 (dog/Life On White/Photodisc), 18 (Jonathon Trappe distant
view/Barcroft Media), 18 (Jonathon Trappe close-up/Barcroft Media), 21 (blind
driver/Photonica/Shelley Wood), 32 (boy/Camille Tokerud/The Image Bank),
32 (woman/Glowimages), 35 (walk/Sean Murphy/Stone+), 37 (Frankie/Gregory
Costanzo/Photodisc), 37 (Isabel/Ivan Jones/The Image Bank), 37 (James/Image
Source), 38 (Buenos Aires/Chad Ehlers/Stone), 39 (man/Photodisc), 40 (Michael
Dunning/Photographer's Choice), 41 (AAGAMIA/Iconica), 43 (Picadilly Circus/
Lee Frost/Robert Harding World Imagery), 43 (Trafalgar Square/Rose Horridge),
43 (Westminster Abbey/Datacraft Co Ltd), 46 (man/Fuse), 46 (Mount Kilimajaro/
David Madison/The Image Bank), 48 (Cultura/Howard Kingsnorth/StockImage),
49 (Sean Russell), 51 (woman/Cohen/Ostrow/Digital Vision), 53 (football player/
John Lund/Sam Diephuis/Blend Images), 54 (Design Pics/Darren Greenwood),
57 (helicopter/Image Source), 72 (traffic lights/François Angers/Flickr), 74 (man/
George Doyle/Stockbyte), 74 (Greece background/Diane Cook and Len Jenshel/
The Image Bank), 74 (woman/Ghislain & Marie David de Lossy/Cultura),
76 (woman/Kactus/StockImage), 77 (Jean Baptiste Lacroix/FilmMagic), 79 (The
Rolling Stones 1960s/Robert Knight Archive/Redferns), 79 (The Rolling Stones
today/SASCHA SCHUERMANN/AFP), 82 (Comstock), 83 (man/Monty Rakusen/
Cultura), 87 (Inti St Clair/Blend Images); iStockphoto pp.39 (woman/4x6),
43 (Tower Bridge/Sergey Borisov), 67 (battery/PashaIgnatov), 68 (Jan Rihak),
71 (Cathy/Florea Marius Catalin), 71 (Michelle/drbimages), 71 (Adrian/Lisa
Svara), 71 (Shona/Tom Fullum), 72 (headphones/Svetlana Gryankina), 85 (Robert/
Joan Vicent Cantó Roig), 85 (Sonia/Cameron Whitman), 85 (Harry/Joan Vicent
Cantó Roig), 85 (Lucy/Joan Vicent Cantó Roig); NI Syndication p.70 (Mary Turner/
The Times); Rex Features pp.67 (accident/Geoff Moore), 72 (traffic jam/Palash
Khan), 86 (United National Photographers); SWNS.COM p.36; Tameside Local
Studies and Archives Centre, Ashton-under-Lyne p.29 (Mr Lees's restaurant)

*The authors and publisher are grateful to those who have given permission to reproduce
the following extracts and adaptations of copyright material*: p.36 'The refugee from
Afghanistan'. Reproduced by kind permission of Mohammad Razai; p.64
'Things we never said' by Fiona Goble. Reproduced by kind permission;
p.67 'Scientists develop mobile phone battery that can be charged in just 10
seconds' by David Derbyshire, from www.dailymail.co.uk 11 March 2009.
Reproduced by kind permission of Solo Syndication; p.77 Fictititous interview
with Juliette Binoche. Reprinted by kind permission of INTERTALENT on
behalf of Juliette Binoche; p.85 'Close your eyes. I'm going to show you the
meaning of life' by David Flusfeder, originally published in Live Magazine,
19 June 2011. Reproduced by kind permission.

*Although every effort has been made to trace and contact copyright holders before
publication, this has not been possible in some cases. We apologize for any apparent
infringement of copyright and if notified, the publisher will be pleased to rectify any
errors or omissions at the earliest opportunity.*

*Sources*: p.22 The Daily Mail